C-2329   CAREER EXAMINATION SERIES

This is your
PASSBOOK for...

Medical Record Technician

Test Preparation Study Guide
Questions & Answers

COPYRIGHT NOTICE

This book is SOLELY intended for, is sold ONLY to, and its use is RESTRICTED to individual, bona fide applicants or candidates who qualify by virtue of having seriously filed applications for appropriate license, certificate, professional and/or promotional advancement, higher school matriculation, scholarship, or other legitimate requirements of education and/or governmental authorities.

This book is NOT intended for use, class instruction, tutoring, training, duplication, copying, reprinting, excerption, or adaptation, etc., by:

1) Other publishers
2) Proprietors and/or Instructors of "Coaching" and/or Preparatory Courses
3) Personnel and/or Training Divisions of commercial, industrial, and governmental organizations
4) Schools, colleges, or universities and/or their departments and staffs, including teachers and other personnel
5) Testing Agencies or Bureaus
6) Study groups which seek by the purchase of a single volume to copy and/or duplicate and/or adapt this material for use by the group as a whole without having purchased individual volumes for each of the members of the group
7) Et al.

Such persons would be in violation of appropriate Federal and State statutes.

PROVISION OF LICENSING AGREEMENTS – Recognized educational, commercial, industrial, and governmental institutions and organizations, and others legitimately engaged in educational pursuits, including training, testing, and measurement activities, may address request for a licensing agreement to the copyright owners, who will determine whether, and under what conditions, including fees and charges, the materials in this book may be used them. In other words, a licensing facility exists for the legitimate use of the material in this book on other than an individual basis. However, it is asseverated and affirmed here that the material in this book CANNOT be used without the receipt of the express permission of such a licensing agreement from the Publishers. Inquiries re licensing should be addressed to the company, attention rights and permissions department.

All rights reserved, including the right of reproduction in whole or in part, in any form or by any means, electronic or mechanical, including photocopying, recording, or by any information storage and retrieval system, without permission in writing from the Publisher.

Copyright © 2025 by
National Learning Corporation

212 Michael Drive, Syosset, NY 11791
(516) 921-8888 • www.passbooks.com
E-mail: info@passbooks.com

PASSBOOK® SERIES

THE *PASSBOOK® SERIES* has been created to prepare applicants and candidates for the ultimate academic battlefield – the examination room.

At some time in our lives, each and every one of us may be required to take an examination – for validation, matriculation, admission, qualification, registration, certification, or licensure.

Based on the assumption that every applicant or candidate has met the basic formal educational standards, has taken the required number of courses, and read the necessary texts, the *PASSBOOK® SERIES* furnishes the one special preparation which may assure passing with confidence, instead of failing with insecurity. Examination questions – together with answers – are furnished as the basic vehicle for study so that the mysteries of the examination and its compounding difficulties may be eliminated or diminished by a sure method.

This book is meant to help you pass your examination provided that you qualify and are serious in your objective.

The entire field is reviewed through the huge store of content information which is succinctly presented through a provocative and challenging approach – the question-and-answer method.

A climate of success is established by furnishing the correct answers at the end of each test.

You soon learn to recognize types of questions, forms of questions, and patterns of questioning. You may even begin to anticipate expected outcomes.

You perceive that many questions are repeated or adapted so that you can gain acute insights, which may enable you to score many sure points.

You learn how to confront new questions, or types of questions, and to attack them confidently and work out the correct answers.

You note objectives and emphases, and recognize pitfalls and dangers, so that you may make positive educational adjustments.

Moreover, you are kept fully informed in relation to new concepts, methods, practices, and directions in the field.

You discover that you are actually taking the examination all the time: you are preparing for the examination by "taking" an examination, not by reading extraneous and/or supererogatory textbooks.

In short, this PASSBOOK®, used directedly, should be an important factor in helping you to pass your test.

MEDICAL RECORD TECHNICIAN

DUTIES
Participates in the classification, cross-indexing, and filing of medical records and documents; performs related duties as required.

SUBJECT OF EXAMINATION
The written test will be designed to test for knowledge, skills, and/or abilities in such areas as:
1. Coding and indexing according to the International Classification of Diseases;
2. Medical terminology including terminology relating to human anatomy and physiology; and
3. Medical record science.

HOW TO TAKE A TEST

I. YOU MUST PASS AN EXAMINATION

A. WHAT EVERY CANDIDATE SHOULD KNOW

Examination applicants often ask us for help in preparing for the written test. What can I study in advance? What kinds of questions will be asked? How will the test be given? How will the papers be graded?

As an applicant for a civil service examination, you may be wondering about some of these things. Our purpose here is to suggest effective methods of advance study and to describe civil service examinations.

Your chances for success on this examination can be increased if you know how to prepare. Those "pre-examination jitters" can be reduced if you know what to expect. You can even experience an adventure in good citizenship if you know why civil service exams are given.

B. WHY ARE CIVIL SERVICE EXAMINATIONS GIVEN?

Civil service examinations are important to you in two ways. As a citizen, you want public jobs filled by employees who know how to do their work. As a job seeker, you want a fair chance to compete for that job on an equal footing with other candidates. The best-known means of accomplishing this two-fold goal is the competitive examination.

Exams are widely publicized throughout the nation. They may be administered for jobs in federal, state, city, municipal, town or village governments or agencies.

Any citizen may apply, with some limitations, such as the age or residence of applicants. Your experience and education may be reviewed to see whether you meet the requirements for the particular examination. When these requirements exist, they are reasonable and applied consistently to all applicants. Thus, a competitive examination may cause you some uneasiness now, but it is your privilege and safeguard.

C. HOW ARE CIVIL SERVICE EXAMS DEVELOPED?

Examinations are carefully written by trained technicians who are specialists in the field known as "psychological measurement," in consultation with recognized authorities in the field of work that the test will cover. These experts recommend the subject matter areas or skills to be tested; only those knowledges or skills important to your success on the job are included. The most reliable books and source materials available are used as references. Together, the experts and technicians judge the difficulty level of the questions.

Test technicians know how to phrase questions so that the problem is clearly stated. Their ethics do not permit "trick" or "catch" questions. Questions may have been tried out on sample groups, or subjected to statistical analysis, to determine their usefulness.

Written tests are often used in combination with performance tests, ratings of training and experience, and oral interviews. All of these measures combine to form the best-known means of finding the right person for the right job.

II. HOW TO PASS THE WRITTEN TEST

A. NATURE OF THE EXAMINATION

To prepare intelligently for civil service examinations, you should know how they differ from school examinations you have taken. In school you were assigned certain definite pages to read or subjects to cover. The examination questions were quite detailed and usually emphasized memory. Civil service exams, on the other hand, try to discover your present ability to perform the duties of a position, plus your potentiality to learn these duties. In other words, a civil service exam attempts to predict how successful you will be. Questions cover such a broad area that they cannot be as minute and detailed as school exam questions.

In the public service similar kinds of work, or positions, are grouped together in one "class." This process is known as *position-classification*. All the positions in a class are paid according to the salary range for that class. One class title covers all of these positions, and they are all tested by the same examination.

B. FOUR BASIC STEPS

1) Study the announcement

How, then, can you know what subjects to study? Our best answer is: "Learn as much as possible about the class of positions for which you've applied." The exam will test the knowledge, skills and abilities needed to do the work.

Your most valuable source of information about the position you want is the official exam announcement. This announcement lists the training and experience qualifications. Check these standards and apply only if you come reasonably close to meeting them.

The brief description of the position in the examination announcement offers some clues to the subjects which will be tested. Think about the job itself. Review the duties in your mind. Can you perform them, or are there some in which you are rusty? Fill in the blank spots in your preparation.

Many jurisdictions preview the written test in the exam announcement by including a section called "Knowledge and Abilities Required," "Scope of the Examination," or some similar heading. Here you will find out specifically what fields will be tested.

2) Review your own background

Once you learn in general what the position is all about, and what you need to know to do the work, ask yourself which subjects you already know fairly well and which need improvement. You may wonder whether to concentrate on improving your strong areas or on building some background in your fields of weakness. When the announcement has specified "some knowledge" or "considerable knowledge," or has used adjectives like "beginning principles of…" or "advanced … methods," you can get a clue as to the number and difficulty of questions to be asked in any given field. More questions, and hence broader coverage, would be included for those subjects which are more important in the work. Now weigh your strengths and weaknesses against the job requirements and prepare accordingly.

3) Determine the level of the position

Another way to tell how intensively you should prepare is to understand the level of the job for which you are applying. Is it the entering level? In other words, is this the position in which beginners in a field of work are hired? Or is it an intermediate or advanced level? Sometimes this is indicated by such words as "Junior" or "Senior" in the class title. Other jurisdictions use Roman numerals to designate the level – Clerk I, Clerk II, for example. The word "Supervisor" sometimes appears in the title. If the level is not indicated by the title, check the description of duties. Will you be working under very close supervision, or will you have responsibility for independent decisions in this work?

4) Choose appropriate study materials

Now that you know the subjects to be examined and the relative amount of each subject to be covered, you can choose suitable study materials. For beginning level jobs, or even advanced ones, if you have a pronounced weakness in some aspect of your training, read a modern, standard textbook in that field. Be sure it is up to date and has general coverage. Such books are normally available at your library, and the librarian will be glad to help you locate one. For entry-level positions, questions of appropriate difficulty are chosen – neither highly advanced questions, nor those too simple. Such questions require careful thought but not advanced training.

If the position for which you are applying is technical or advanced, you will read more advanced, specialized material. If you are already familiar with the basic principles of your field, elementary textbooks would waste your time. Concentrate on advanced textbooks and technical periodicals. Think through the concepts and review difficult problems in your field.

These are all general sources. You can get more ideas on your own initiative, following these leads. For example, training manuals and publications of the government agency which employs workers in your field can be useful, particularly for technical and professional positions. A letter or visit to the government department involved may result in more specific study suggestions, and certainly will provide you with a more definite idea of the exact nature of the position you are seeking.

III. KINDS OF TESTS

Tests are used for purposes other than measuring knowledge and ability to perform specified duties. For some positions, it is equally important to test ability to make adjustments to new situations or to profit from training. In others, basic mental abilities not dependent on information are essential. Questions which test these things may not appear as pertinent to the duties of the position as those which test for knowledge and information. Yet they are often highly important parts of a fair examination. For very general questions, it is almost impossible to help you direct your study efforts. What we can do is to point out some of the more common of these general abilities needed in public service positions and describe some typical questions.

1) General information

Broad, general information has been found useful for predicting job success in some kinds of work. This is tested in a variety of ways, from vocabulary lists to questions about current events. Basic background in some field of work, such as sociology or economics, may be sampled in a group of questions. Often these are principles which have become familiar to most persons through exposure rather than through formal training. It is difficult to advise you how to study for these questions; being alert to the world around you is our best suggestion.

2) Verbal ability

An example of an ability needed in many positions is verbal or language ability. Verbal ability is, in brief, the ability to use and understand words. Vocabulary and grammar tests are typical measures of this ability. Reading comprehension or paragraph interpretation questions are common in many kinds of civil service tests. You are given a paragraph of written material and asked to find its central meaning.

3) Numerical ability

Number skills can be tested by the familiar arithmetic problem, by checking paired lists of numbers to see which are alike and which are different, or by interpreting charts and graphs. In the latter test, a graph may be printed in the test booklet which you are asked to use as the basis for answering questions.

4) Observation

A popular test for law-enforcement positions is the observation test. A picture is shown to you for several minutes, then taken away. Questions about the picture test your ability to observe both details and larger elements.

5) Following directions

In many positions in the public service, the employee must be able to carry out written instructions dependably and accurately. You may be given a chart with several columns, each column listing a variety of information. The questions require you to carry out directions involving the information given in the chart.

6) Skills and aptitudes

Performance tests effectively measure some manual skills and aptitudes. When the skill is one in which you are trained, such as typing or shorthand, you can practice. These tests are often very much like those given in business school or high school courses. For many of the other skills and aptitudes, however, no short-time preparation can be made. Skills and abilities natural to you or that you have developed throughout your lifetime are being tested.

Many of the general questions just described provide all the data needed to answer the questions and ask you to use your reasoning ability to find the answers. Your best preparation for these tests, as well as for tests of facts and ideas, is to be at your physical and mental best. You, no doubt, have your own methods of getting into an exam-taking mood and keeping "in shape." The next section lists some ideas on this subject.

IV. KINDS OF QUESTIONS

Only rarely is the "essay" question, which you answer in narrative form, used in civil service tests. Civil service tests are usually of the short-answer type. Full instructions for answering these questions will be given to you at the examination. But in case this is your first experience with short-answer questions and separate answer sheets, here is what you need to know:

1) **Multiple-choice Questions**

Most popular of the short-answer questions is the "multiple choice" or "best answer" question. It can be used, for example, to test for factual knowledge, ability to solve problems or judgment in meeting situations found at work.

A multiple-choice question is normally one of three types—
- It can begin with an incomplete statement followed by several possible endings. You are to find the one ending which *best* completes the statement, although some of the others may not be entirely wrong.
- It can also be a complete statement in the form of a question which is answered by choosing one of the statements listed.

- It can be in the form of a problem – again you select the best answer.

Here is an example of a multiple-choice question with a discussion which should give you some clues as to the method for choosing the right answer:

When an employee has a complaint about his assignment, the action which will *best* help him overcome his difficulty is to
- A. discuss his difficulty with his coworkers
- B. take the problem to the head of the organization
- C. take the problem to the person who gave him the assignment
- D. say nothing to anyone about his complaint

In answering this question, you should study each of the choices to find which is best. Consider choice "A" – Certainly an employee may discuss his complaint with fellow employees, but no change or improvement can result, and the complaint remains unresolved. Choice "B" is a poor choice since the head of the organization probably does not know what assignment you have been given, and taking your problem to him is known as "going over the head" of the supervisor. The supervisor, or person who made the assignment, is the person who can clarify it or correct any injustice. Choice "C" is, therefore, correct. To say nothing, as in choice "D," is unwise. Supervisors have and interest in knowing the problems employees are facing, and the employee is seeking a solution to his problem.

2) True/False Questions

The "true/false" or "right/wrong" form of question is sometimes used. Here a complete statement is given. Your job is to decide whether the statement is right or wrong.

SAMPLE: A roaming cell-phone call to a nearby city costs less than a non-roaming call to a distant city.

This statement is wrong, or false, since roaming calls are more expensive.

This is not a complete list of all possible question forms, although most of the others are variations of these common types. You will always get complete directions for answering questions. Be sure you understand *how* to mark your answers – ask questions until you do.

V. RECORDING YOUR ANSWERS

Computer terminals are used more and more today for many different kinds of exams.

For an examination with very few applicants, you may be told to record your answers in the test booklet itself. Separate answer sheets are much more common. If this separate answer sheet is to be scored by machine – and this is often the case – it is highly important that you mark your answers correctly in order to get credit.

An electronic scoring machine is often used in civil service offices because of the speed with which papers can be scored. Machine-scored answer sheets must be marked with a pencil, which will be given to you. This pencil has a high graphite content which responds to the electronic scoring machine. As a matter of fact, stray dots may register as answers, so do not let your pencil rest on the answer sheet while you are pondering the correct answer. Also, if your pencil lead breaks or is otherwise defective, ask for another.

Since the answer sheet will be dropped in a slot in the scoring machine, be careful not to bend the corners or get the paper crumpled.

The answer sheet normally has five vertical columns of numbers, with 30 numbers to a column. These numbers correspond to the question numbers in your test booklet. After each number, going across the page are four or five pairs of dotted lines. These short dotted lines have small letters or numbers above them. The first two pairs may also have a "T" or "F" above the letters. This indicates that the first two pairs only are to be used if the questions are of the true-false type. If the questions are multiple choice, disregard the "T" and "F" and pay attention only to the small letters or numbers.

Answer your questions in the manner of the sample that follows:

32. The largest city in the United States is
    A. Washington, D.C.
    B. New York City
    C. Chicago
    D. Detroit
    E. San Francisco

1) Choose the answer you think is best. (New York City is the largest, so "B" is correct.)
2) Find the row of dotted lines numbered the same as the question you are answering. (Find row number 32)
3) Find the pair of dotted lines corresponding to the answer. (Find the pair of lines under the mark "B.")
4) Make a solid black mark between the dotted lines.

VI. BEFORE THE TEST

Common sense will help you find procedures to follow to get ready for an examination. Too many of us, however, overlook these sensible measures. Indeed, nervousness and fatigue have been found to be the most serious reasons why applicants fail to do their best on civil service tests. Here is a list of reminders:

- Begin your preparation early – Don't wait until the last minute to go scurrying around for books and materials or to find out what the position is all about.
- Prepare continuously – An hour a night for a week is better than an all-night cram session. This has been definitely established. What is more, a night a week for a month will return better dividends than crowding your study into a shorter period of time.
- Locate the place of the exam – You have been sent a notice telling you when and where to report for the examination. If the location is in a different town or otherwise unfamiliar to you, it would be well to inquire the best route and learn something about the building.
- Relax the night before the test – Allow your mind to rest. Do not study at all that night. Plan some mild recreation or diversion; then go to bed early and get a good night's sleep.
- Get up early enough to make a leisurely trip to the place for the test – This way unforeseen events, traffic snarls, unfamiliar buildings, etc. will not upset you.
- Dress comfortably – A written test is not a fashion show. You will be known by number and not by name, so wear something comfortable.

- Leave excess paraphernalia at home – Shopping bags and odd bundles will get in your way. You need bring only the items mentioned in the official notice you received; usually everything you need is provided. Do not bring reference books to the exam. They will only confuse those last minutes and be taken away from you when in the test room.
- Arrive somewhat ahead of time – If because of transportation schedules you must get there very early, bring a newspaper or magazine to take your mind off yourself while waiting.
- Locate the examination room – When you have found the proper room, you will be directed to the seat or part of the room where you will sit. Sometimes you are given a sheet of instructions to read while you are waiting. Do not fill out any forms until you are told to do so; just read them and be prepared.
- Relax and prepare to listen to the instructions
- If you have any physical problem that may keep you from doing your best, be sure to tell the test administrator. If you are sick or in poor health, you really cannot do your best on the exam. You can come back and take the test some other time.

VII. AT THE TEST

The day of the test is here and you have the test booklet in your hand. The temptation to get going is very strong. Caution! There is more to success than knowing the right answers. You must know how to identify your papers and understand variations in the type of short-answer question used in this particular examination. Follow these suggestions for maximum results from your efforts:

1) Cooperate with the monitor

The test administrator has a duty to create a situation in which you can be as much at ease as possible. He will give instructions, tell you when to begin, check to see that you are marking your answer sheet correctly, and so on. He is not there to guard you, although he will see that your competitors do not take unfair advantage. He wants to help you do your best.

2) Listen to all instructions

Don't jump the gun! Wait until you understand all directions. In most civil service tests you get more time than you need to answer the questions. So don't be in a hurry. Read each word of instructions until you clearly understand the meaning. Study the examples, listen to all announcements and follow directions. Ask questions if you do not understand what to do.

3) Identify your papers

Civil service exams are usually identified by number only. You will be assigned a number; you must not put your name on your test papers. Be sure to copy your number correctly. Since more than one exam may be given, copy your exact examination title.

4) Plan your time

Unless you are told that a test is a "speed" or "rate of work" test, speed itself is usually not important. Time enough to answer all the questions will be provided, but this does not mean that you have all day. An overall time limit has been set. Divide the total time (in minutes) by the number of questions to determine the approximate time you have for each question.

5) Do not linger over difficult questions

If you come across a difficult question, mark it with a paper clip (useful to have along) and come back to it when you have been through the booklet. One caution if you do this – be sure to skip a number on your answer sheet as well. Check often to be sure that you have not lost your place and that you are marking in the row numbered the same as the question you are answering.

6) Read the questions

Be sure you know what the question asks! Many capable people are unsuccessful because they failed to *read* the questions correctly.

7) Answer all questions

Unless you have been instructed that a penalty will be deducted for incorrect answers, it is better to guess than to omit a question.

8) Speed tests

It is often better NOT to guess on speed tests. It has been found that on timed tests people are tempted to spend the last few seconds before time is called in marking answers at random – without even reading them – in the hope of picking up a few extra points. To discourage this practice, the instructions may warn you that your score will be "corrected" for guessing. That is, a penalty will be applied. The incorrect answers will be deducted from the correct ones, or some other penalty formula will be used.

9) Review your answers

If you finish before time is called, go back to the questions you guessed or omitted to give them further thought. Review other answers if you have time.

10) Return your test materials

If you are ready to leave before others have finished or time is called, take ALL your materials to the monitor and leave quietly. Never take any test material with you. The monitor can discover whose papers are not complete, and taking a test booklet may be grounds for disqualification.

VIII. EXAMINATION TECHNIQUES

1) Read the general instructions carefully. These are usually printed on the first page of the exam booklet. As a rule, these instructions refer to the timing of the examination; the fact that you should not start work until the signal and must stop work at a signal, etc. If there are any *special* instructions, such as a choice of questions to be answered, make sure that you note this instruction carefully.

2) When you are ready to start work on the examination, that is as soon as the signal has been given, read the instructions to each question booklet, underline any key words or phrases, such as *least, best, outline, describe* and the like. In this way you will tend to answer as requested rather than discover on reviewing your paper that you *listed without describing*, that you selected the *worst* choice rather than the *best* choice, etc.

3) If the examination is of the objective or multiple-choice type – that is, each question will also give a series of possible answers: A, B, C or D, and you are called upon to select the best answer and write the letter next to that answer on your answer paper – it is advisable to start answering each question in turn. There may be anywhere from 50 to 100 such questions in the three or four hours allotted and you can see how much time would be taken if you read through all the questions before beginning to answer any. Furthermore, if you come across a question or group of questions which you know would be difficult to answer, it would undoubtedly affect your handling of all the other questions.

4) If the examination is of the essay type and contains but a few questions, it is a moot point as to whether you should read all the questions before starting to answer any one. Of course, if you are given a choice – say five out of seven and the like – then it is essential to read all the questions so you can eliminate the two that are most difficult. If, however, you are asked to answer all the questions, there may be danger in trying to answer the easiest one first because you may find that you will spend too much time on it. The best technique is to answer the first question, then proceed to the second, etc.

5) Time your answers. Before the exam begins, write down the time it started, then add the time allowed for the examination and write down the time it must be completed, then divide the time available somewhat as follows:
    - If 3-1/2 hours are allowed, that would be 210 minutes. If you have 80 objective-type questions, that would be an average of 2-1/2 minutes per question. Allow yourself no more than 2 minutes per question, or a total of 160 minutes, which will permit about 50 minutes to review.
    - If for the time allotment of 210 minutes there are 7 essay questions to answer, that would average about 30 minutes a question. Give yourself only 25 minutes per question so that you have about 35 minutes to review.

6) The most important instruction is to *read each question* and make sure you know what is wanted. The second most important instruction is to *time yourself properly* so that you answer every question. The third most important instruction is to *answer every question*. Guess if you have to but include something for each question. Remember that you will receive no credit for a blank and will probably receive some credit if you write something in answer to an essay question. If you guess a letter – say "B" for a multiple-choice question – you may have guessed right. If you leave a blank as an answer to a multiple-choice question, the examiners may respect your feelings but it will not add a point to your score. Some exams may penalize you for wrong answers, so in such cases *only*, you may not want to guess unless you have some basis for your answer.

7) Suggestions
    a. Objective-type questions
        1. Examine the question booklet for proper sequence of pages and questions
        2. Read all instructions carefully
        3. Skip any question which seems too difficult; return to it after all other questions have been answered
        4. Apportion your time properly; do not spend too much time on any single question or group of questions

5. Note and underline key words – *all, most, fewest, least, best, worst, same, opposite,* etc.
6. Pay particular attention to negatives
7. Note unusual option, e.g., unduly long, short, complex, different or similar in content to the body of the question
8. Observe the use of "hedging" words – *probably, may, most likely,* etc.
9. Make sure that your answer is put next to the same number as the question
10. Do not second-guess unless you have good reason to believe the second answer is definitely more correct
11. Cross out original answer if you decide another answer is more accurate; do not erase until you are ready to hand your paper in
12. Answer all questions; guess unless instructed otherwise
13. Leave time for review

   b. Essay questions
1. Read each question carefully
2. Determine exactly what is wanted. Underline key words or phrases.
3. Decide on outline or paragraph answer
4. Include many different points and elements unless asked to develop any one or two points or elements
5. Show impartiality by giving pros and cons unless directed to select one side only
6. Make and write down any assumptions you find necessary to answer the questions
7. Watch your English, grammar, punctuation and choice of words
8. Time your answers; don't crowd material

8) Answering the essay question

Most essay questions can be answered by framing the specific response around several key words or ideas. Here are a few such key words or ideas:

M's: manpower, materials, methods, money, management
P's: purpose, program, policy, plan, procedure, practice, problems, pitfalls, personnel, public relations

   a. Six basic steps in handling problems:
1. Preliminary plan and background development
2. Collect information, data and facts
3. Analyze and interpret information, data and facts
4. Analyze and develop solutions as well as make recommendations
5. Prepare report and sell recommendations
6. Install recommendations and follow up effectiveness

   b. Pitfalls to avoid
1. *Taking things for granted* – A statement of the situation does not necessarily imply that each of the elements is necessarily true; for example, a complaint may be invalid and biased so that all that can be taken for granted is that a complaint has been registered

2. *Considering only one side of a situation* – Wherever possible, indicate several alternatives and then point out the reasons you selected the best one
3. *Failing to indicate follow up* – Whenever your answer indicates action on your part, make certain that you will take proper follow-up action to see how successful your recommendations, procedures or actions turn out to be
4. *Taking too long in answering any single question* – Remember to time your answers properly

IX. AFTER THE TEST

Scoring procedures differ in detail among civil service jurisdictions although the general principles are the same. Whether the papers are hand-scored or graded by machine we have described, they are nearly always graded by number. That is, the person who marks the paper knows only the number – never the name – of the applicant. Not until all the papers have been graded will they be matched with names. If other tests, such as training and experience or oral interview ratings have been given, scores will be combined. Different parts of the examination usually have different weights. For example, the written test might count 60 percent of the final grade, and a rating of training and experience 40 percent. In many jurisdictions, veterans will have a certain number of points added to their grades.

After the final grade has been determined, the names are placed in grade order and an eligible list is established. There are various methods for resolving ties between those who get the same final grade – probably the most common is to place first the name of the person whose application was received first. Job offers are made from the eligible list in the order the names appear on it. You will be notified of your grade and your rank as soon as all these computations have been made. This will be done as rapidly as possible.

People who are found to meet the requirements in the announcement are called "eligibles." Their names are put on a list of eligible candidates. An eligible's chances of getting a job depend on how high he stands on this list and how fast agencies are filling jobs from the list.

When a job is to be filled from a list of eligibles, the agency asks for the names of people on the list of eligibles for that job. When the civil service commission receives this request, it sends to the agency the names of the three people highest on this list. Or, if the job to be filled has specialized requirements, the office sends the agency the names of the top three persons who meet these requirements from the general list.

The appointing officer makes a choice from among the three people whose names were sent to him. If the selected person accepts the appointment, the names of the others are put back on the list to be considered for future openings.

That is the rule in hiring from all kinds of eligible lists, whether they are for typist, carpenter, chemist, or something else. For every vacancy, the appointing officer has his choice of any one of the top three eligibles on the list. This explains why the person whose name is on top of the list sometimes does not get an appointment when some of the persons lower on the list do. If the appointing officer chooses the second or third eligible, the No. 1 eligible does not get a job at once, but stays on the list until he is appointed or the list is terminated.

X. HOW TO PASS THE INTERVIEW TEST

The examination for which you applied requires an oral interview test. You have already taken the written test and you are now being called for the interview test – the final part of the formal examination.

You may think that it is not possible to prepare for an interview test and that there are no procedures to follow during an interview. Our purpose is to point out some things you can do in advance that will help you and some good rules to follow and pitfalls to avoid while you are being interviewed.

What is an interview supposed to test?

The written examination is designed to test the technical knowledge and competence of the candidate; the oral is designed to evaluate intangible qualities, not readily measured otherwise, and to establish a list showing the relative fitness of each candidate – as measured against his competitors – for the position sought. Scoring is not on the basis of "right" and "wrong," but on a sliding scale of values ranging from "not passable" to "outstanding." As a matter of fact, it is possible to achieve a relatively low score without a single "incorrect" answer because of evident weakness in the qualities being measured.

Occasionally, an examination may consist entirely of an oral test – either an individual or a group oral. In such cases, information is sought concerning the technical knowledges and abilities of the candidate, since there has been no written examination for this purpose. More commonly, however, an oral test is used to supplement a written examination.

Who conducts interviews?

The composition of oral boards varies among different jurisdictions. In nearly all, a representative of the personnel department serves as chairman. One of the members of the board may be a representative of the department in which the candidate would work. In some cases, "outside experts" are used, and, frequently, a businessman or some other representative of the general public is asked to serve. Labor and management or other special groups may be represented. The aim is to secure the services of experts in the appropriate field.

However the board is composed, it is a good idea (and not at all improper or unethical) to ascertain in advance of the interview who the members are and what groups they represent. When you are introduced to them, you will have some idea of their backgrounds and interests, and at least you will not stutter and stammer over their names.

What should be done before the interview?

While knowledge about the board members is useful and takes some of the surprise element out of the interview, there is other preparation which is more substantive. It *is* possible to prepare for an oral interview – in several ways:

1) Keep a copy of your application and review it carefully before the interview

This may be the only document before the oral board, and the starting point of the interview. Know what education and experience you have listed there, and the sequence and dates of all of it. Sometimes the board will ask you to review the highlights of your experience for them; you should not have to hem and haw doing it.

2) Study the class specification and the examination announcement

Usually, the oral board has one or both of these to guide them. The qualities, characteristics or knowledges required by the position sought are stated in these documents. They offer valuable clues as to the nature of the oral interview. For example, if the job involves supervisory responsibilities, the announcement will usually indicate that knowledge of modern supervisory methods and the qualifications of the candidate as a supervisor will be tested. If so, you can expect such questions, frequently in the form of a hypothetical situation which you are expected to solve. NEVER go into an oral without knowledge of the duties and responsibilities of the job you seek.

3) Think through each qualification required

Try to visualize the kind of questions you would ask if you were a board member. How well could you answer them? Try especially to appraise your own knowledge and background in each area, *measured against the job sought*, and identify any areas in which you are weak. Be critical and realistic – do not flatter yourself.

4) Do some general reading in areas in which you feel you may be weak

For example, if the job involves supervision and your past experience has NOT, some general reading in supervisory methods and practices, particularly in the field of human relations, might be useful. Do NOT study agency procedures or detailed manuals. The oral board will be testing your understanding and capacity, not your memory.

5) Get a good night's sleep and watch your general health and mental attitude

You will want a clear head at the interview. Take care of a cold or any other minor ailment, and of course, no hangovers.

What should be done on the day of the interview?

Now comes the day of the interview itself. Give yourself plenty of time to get there. Plan to arrive somewhat ahead of the scheduled time, particularly if your appointment is in the fore part of the day. If a previous candidate fails to appear, the board might be ready for you a bit early. By early afternoon an oral board is almost invariably behind schedule if there are many candidates, and you may have to wait. Take along a book or magazine to read, or your application to review, but leave any extraneous material in the waiting room when you go in for your interview. In any event, relax and compose yourself.

The matter of dress is important. The board is forming impressions about you – from your experience, your manners, your attitude, and your appearance. Give your personal appearance careful attention. Dress your best, but not your flashiest. Choose conservative, appropriate clothing, and be sure it is immaculate. This is a business interview, and your appearance should indicate that you regard it as such. Besides, being well groomed and properly dressed will help boost your confidence.

Sooner or later, someone will call your name and escort you into the interview room. *This is it.* From here on you are on your own. It is too late for any more preparation. But remember, you asked for this opportunity to prove your fitness, and you are here because your request was granted.

What happens when you go in?

The usual sequence of events will be as follows: The clerk (who is often the board stenographer) will introduce you to the chairman of the oral board, who will introduce you to the other members of the board. Acknowledge the introductions before you sit down. Do not be surprised if you find a microphone facing you or a stenotypist sitting by. Oral interviews are usually recorded in the event of an appeal or other review.

Usually the chairman of the board will open the interview by reviewing the highlights of your education and work experience from your application – primarily for the benefit of the other members of the board, as well as to get the material into the record. Do not interrupt or comment unless there is an error or significant misinterpretation; if that is the case, do not hesitate. But do not quibble about insignificant matters. Also, he will usually ask you some question about your education, experience or your present job – partly to get you to start talking and to establish the interviewing "rapport." He may start the actual questioning, or turn it over to one of the other members. Frequently, each member undertakes the questioning on a particular area, one in which he is perhaps most competent, so you can expect each member to participate in the examination. Because time is limited, you may also expect some rather abrupt switches in the direction the questioning takes, so do not be upset by it. Normally, a board member will not pursue a single line of questioning unless he discovers a particular strength or weakness.

After each member has participated, the chairman will usually ask whether any member has any further questions, then will ask you if you have anything you wish to add. Unless you are expecting this question, it may floor you. Worse, it may start you off on an extended, extemporaneous speech. The board is not usually seeking more information. The question is principally to offer you a last opportunity to present further qualifications or to indicate that you have nothing to add. So, if you feel that a significant qualification or characteristic has been overlooked, it is proper to point it out in a sentence or so. Do not compliment the board on the thoroughness of their examination – they have been sketchy, and you know it. If you wish, merely say, "No thank you, I have nothing further to add." This is a point where you can "talk yourself out" of a good impression or fail to present an important bit of information. Remember, *you close the interview yourself.*

The chairman will then say, "That is all, Mr. _____, thank you." Do not be startled; the interview is over, and quicker than you think. Thank him, gather your belongings and take your leave. Save your sigh of relief for the other side of the door.

How to put your best foot forward

Throughout this entire process, you may feel that the board individually and collectively is trying to pierce your defenses, seek out your hidden weaknesses and embarrass and confuse you. Actually, this is not true. They are obliged to make an appraisal of your qualifications for the job you are seeking, and they want to see you in your best light. Remember, they must interview all candidates and a non-cooperative candidate may become a failure in spite of their best efforts to bring out his qualifications. Here are 15 suggestions that will help you:

1) Be natural – Keep your attitude confident, not cocky

If you are not confident that you can do the job, do not expect the board to be. Do not apologize for your weaknesses, try to bring out your strong points. The board is interested in a positive, not negative, presentation. Cockiness will antagonize any board member and make him wonder if you are covering up a weakness by a false show of strength.

2) Get comfortable, but don't lounge or sprawl

Sit erectly but not stiffly. A careless posture may lead the board to conclude that you are careless in other things, or at least that you are not impressed by the importance of the occasion. Either conclusion is natural, even if incorrect. Do not fuss with your clothing, a pencil or an ashtray. Your hands may occasionally be useful to emphasize a point; do not let them become a point of distraction.

3) Do not wisecrack or make small talk

This is a serious situation, and your attitude should show that you consider it as such. Further, the time of the board is limited – they do not want to waste it, and neither should you.

4) Do not exaggerate your experience or abilities

In the first place, from information in the application or other interviews and sources, the board may know more about you than you think. Secondly, you probably will not get away with it. An experienced board is rather adept at spotting such a situation, so do not take the chance.

5) If you know a board member, do not make a point of it, yet do not hide it

Certainly you are not fooling him, and probably not the other members of the board. Do not try to take advantage of your acquaintanceship – it will probably do you little good.

6) Do not dominate the interview

Let the board do that. They will give you the clues – do not assume that you have to do all the talking. Realize that the board has a number of questions to ask you, and do not try to take up all the interview time by showing off your extensive knowledge of the answer to the first one.

7) Be attentive

You only have 20 minutes or so, and you should keep your attention at its sharpest throughout. When a member is addressing a problem or question to you, give him your undivided attention. Address your reply principally to him, but do not exclude the other board members.

8) Do not interrupt

A board member may be stating a problem for you to analyze. He will ask you a question when the time comes. Let him state the problem, and wait for the question.

9) Make sure you understand the question

Do not try to answer until you are sure what the question is. If it is not clear, restate it in your own words or ask the board member to clarify it for you. However, do not haggle about minor elements.

10) Reply promptly but not hastily

A common entry on oral board rating sheets is "candidate responded readily," or "candidate hesitated in replies." Respond as promptly and quickly as you can, but do not jump to a hasty, ill-considered answer.

11) Do not be peremptory in your answers

A brief answer is proper – but do not fire your answer back. That is a losing game from your point of view. The board member can probably ask questions much faster than you can answer them.

12) Do not try to create the answer you think the board member wants

He is interested in what kind of mind you have and how it works – not in playing games. Furthermore, he can usually spot this practice and will actually grade you down on it.

13) Do not switch sides in your reply merely to agree with a board member

Frequently, a member will take a contrary position merely to draw you out and to see if you are willing and able to defend your point of view. Do not start a debate, yet do not surrender a good position. If a position is worth taking, it is worth defending.

14) Do not be afraid to admit an error in judgment if you are shown to be wrong

The board knows that you are forced to reply without any opportunity for careful consideration. Your answer may be demonstrably wrong. If so, admit it and get on with the interview.

15) Do not dwell at length on your present job

The opening question may relate to your present assignment. Answer the question but do not go into an extended discussion. You are being examined for a *new* job, not your present one. As a matter of fact, try to phrase ALL your answers in terms of the job for which you are being examined.

Basis of Rating

Probably you will forget most of these "do's" and "don'ts" when you walk into the oral interview room. Even remembering them all will not ensure you a passing grade. Perhaps you did not have the qualifications in the first place. But remembering them will help you to put your best foot forward, without treading on the toes of the board members.

Rumor and popular opinion to the contrary notwithstanding, an oral board wants you to make the best appearance possible. They know you are under pressure – but they also want to see how you respond to it as a guide to what your reaction would be under the pressures of the job you seek. They will be influenced by the degree of poise you display, the personal traits you show and the manner in which you respond.

ABOUT THIS BOOK

This book contains tests divided into Examination Sections. Go through each test, answering every question in the margin. We have also attached a sample answer sheet at the back of the book that can be removed and used. At the end of each test look at the answer key and check your answers. On the ones you got wrong, look at the right answer choice and learn. Do not fill in the answers first. Do not memorize the questions and answers, but understand the answer and principles involved. On your test, the questions will likely be different from the samples. Questions are changed and new ones added. If you understand these past questions you should have success with any changes that arise. Tests may consist of several types of questions. We have additional books on each subject should more study be advisable or necessary for you. Finally, the more you study, the better prepared you will be. This book is intended to be the last thing you study before you walk into the examination room. Prior study of relevant texts is also recommended. NLC publishes some of these in our Fundamental Series. Knowledge and good sense are important factors in passing your exam. Good luck also helps. So now study this Passbook, absorb the material contained within and take that knowledge into the examination. Then do your best to pass that exam.

EXAMINATION SECTION

EXAMINATION SECTION
TEST 1

DIRECTIONS: Each question or incomplete statement is followed by several suggested answers or completions. Select the one that BEST answers the question or completes the statement. *PRINT THE LETTER OF THE CORRECT ANSWER IN THE SPACE AT THE RIGHT.*

1. Given the standard methods of forms analysis in health information departments, it is usually sufficient to order a supply of forms that will last _____ months.

    A. 1-3 B. 3-6 C. 6-12 D. 12-18

2. According to the rules of the FLSA (Fair Labor and Standards Act), which of the following positions in the health care department is an *exempt* position?

    A. Coding
    B. Abstracting
    C. Administration
    D. Transcription

3. Which of the following would be considered to be a DISADVANTAGE associated with the use of source-oriented medical records?

    A. Format usually requires additional training of records personnel
    B. Complexity of arrangement makes the record difficult for non-physicians to follow
    C. Format does not facilitate use in acute care facilities
    D. Data from various departments are not integrated in the time sequence

4. The definition of objectives is a MAJOR purpose of the _____ function of management.

    A. controlling
    B. directing
    C. planning
    D. organizing

5. In the _____ HMO, physicians maintain their own medical records yet feed practice data into the HMO for monitoring purposes.

    A. staff model
    B. independent practice
    C. preferred provider
    D. group model or closed

6. Which of the following problems would be considered the MOST serious offense committed by an employee in the department?

    A. Attendance problems
    B. Insubordination
    C. Falsification of employment application
    D. Violation of smoking regulations

7. Of the following methods for measuring work to define a performance standard, _____ is used to establish a standard for new work.

    A. benchmarking
    B. scientific method
    C. work sampling
    D. simulation

8. A disease or operation index would be used administratively to

   A. evaluate the quality of care in the facility
   B. procure data on the utilization of facilities and to establish needs for new equipment, beds, etc. in various departments
   C. determine whether treatment and procedures provided were necessary and appropriate for the diagnosis
   D. accumulate risk management data

9. In a hospital's medical record, the medical history of a patient must be completed within _____ hours of the patient's admission.

   A. 6   B. 12   C. 24   D. 48

10. Which of the following situations would be defined as a *professional contact* according to standard ambulatory health care data practices?
    A(n)

    A. patient receiving services from a supplier
    B. outpatient visiting both a physician's office and a clinic as parts of an individual treatment plan
    C. patient's imaging reports being interpreted when the patient is not physically present by someone other than the referring physician
    D. patient receiving services from a pharmacist

11. In hospitals, computerized R-ADT systems are USUALLY under the control of the _____ department.

    A. admissions   B. nursing
    C. radiology   D. health information

12. Which of the following is a component of managerial decision-making?

    A. Developing alternative solutions to the problem to meet the objective
    B. Collecting complete data about all factors surrounding a problem
    C. Identifying objectives in which change is causing a deviation
    D. Analyzing data fully to understand a problem and how it occurs

13. Which of the following items would appear in the follow-up file of a cancer registry?

    A. Histology
    B. Biopsies
    C. Diagnosis
    D. Radiation/chemotherapy treatments

14. In an inpatient acute care psychiatric facility, a patient's records should be reviewed

    A. daily   B. weekly
    C. monthly   D. annually

15. In the utilization review process, the _____ review would MOST likely be performed by a PRO physician.

    A. preadmission   B. continued stay
    C. discharge   D. retrospective

16. The MAIN advantage in using a straight numeric filing system is

    A. increased production of the clerical staff
    B. easy retrieval of an entire record
    C. accessibility to providers
    D. ease in personnel training

17. A key letter used as a category in the phonetic filing system for a Master Patient Index is

    A. k B. b C. s D. n

18. A final progress note may NOT take the place of a discharge summary in the medical record of

    A. patients with minor problems who are hospitalized less than 48 hours
    B. surgical deliveries
    C. normal newborns
    D. uncomplicated obstetrical deliveries

19. In any research study, which of the following steps would occur LAST?

    A. Research report is prepared
    B. Pilot study is conducted
    C. Data gathering and analysis plans are implemented
    D. Frame of reference is developed

20. A _____ is used by health information management for direct observation of work performed when quality is difficult to quantify?

    A. questionnaire   B. checklist
    C. report   D. audit

21. When interviewing an applicant for a position in the department, _____ questions USUALLY should be avoided.

    A. probing   B. yes/no
    C. situational   D. leading

22. Procedures in the ICD-9-CM classification system are coded as a

    A. series of three-letter units
    B. letter followed by a three-digit number
    C. two-digit number, with one or two decimal digit subcategories
    D. four-digit number, without decimal digits

23. The plan of treatment for home care patients is reviewed by the attending physician and agency personnel at least once every

    A. month   B. 60 days
    C. six months   D. year

24. Which method for measuring work to define a performance standard involves comparing one department to another?

    A. Benchmarking   B. Scientific method
    C. Work sampling   D. Simulation

25. Included in the transfer/referral form for patients in long-term care facilities is the 25.____
    A. treatment plan
    B. estimate of rehabilitative potential
    C. recommended treatment
    D. medical history

KEY (CORRECT ANSWERS)

1. C
2. C
3. D
4. C
5. D

6. C
7. D
8. C
9. C
10. C

11. A
12. A
13. C
14. B
15. D

16. D
17. B
18. B
19. A
20. B

21. D
22. C
23. B
24. A
25. B

TEST 2

DIRECTIONS: Each question or incomplete statement is followed by several suggested answers or completions. Select the one that BEST answers the question or completes the statement. *PRINT THE LETTER OF THE CORRECT ANSWER IN THE SPACE AT THE RIGHT.*

1. Of the following basic methods for the release of authorized information from medical records, _____ should be used as a last resort by health information departments. 1._____

    A. direct access
    B. abstracting information
    C. facsimile transmission
    D. verbal release

2. Which of the following functions and responsibilities would be LEAST likely to be assigned to the committee responsible for medical record review? 2._____

    A. Determination of the record format
    B. Review of records for usefulness in quality assessment activities
    C. Review of records for accuracy in describing patient progress
    D. Imposing disciplinary action on medical staff who submit substandard records

3. A hospital had a total of 21 deaths during September. A total of 650 patients were discharged during the month. What was the hospital's GROSS death rate for September? 3._____

    A. .03%   B. 3%   C. 7%   D. 32%

4. Each of the following is a potential use for the accession file of a cancer registry EXCEPT 4._____

    A. monitoring case identification
    B. auditing the registry file for lost abstracts
    C. abstracting nonanalytical cases
    D. assessing registry workload

5. In the analysis of computerized data systems, systems analysis tools are MOST often used during the _____ phase. 5._____

    A. feasibility
    B. research
    C. implementation
    D. initial investigation

6. To determine the total number of file guides needed for record storage, _____ the total number of records _____. 6._____

    A. multiply; between each guide by the total number of records
    B. divide; by the number of records between each guide
    C. subtract; between each guide from the total number of records, and multiply by the number of shelves
    D. divide; by the number of records between each guide, and multiply by the number of shelves

7. To calculate the delinquency rate of a facility's medical record submissions, divide the total number of _____ by the average number of _____ during a completion period. 7._____

    A. delinquent records, minus the death rate; admissions
    B. delinquent records; admissions

5

C. required records, minus the number of delinquent records; discharges
D. delinquent records; discharges

8. Which of the following is a *vertical* component of work allocation? 8.____

   A. Line-staff responsibility
   B. Departmentalization
   C. Delegation
   D. Coordination

9. According to the alphabetical filing guidelines for entering data into the Master Patient Index, which of the following names would appear FIRST in the Index? 9.____

   A. D'Elba
   B. Di Luca
   C. de Armand
   D. De Smet

10. All of the following would describe techniques used by the APG classification system for grouping different services EXCEPT 10.____

    A. normally scheduled, significant procedures which dominate time and resources expended during a patient visit
    B. multiple significant procedures and ancillary discounting, for multiple unrelated significant procedures, or multiple performance of the same ancillary procedure
    C. ancillary discounting for multiple performance of different ancillary procedures that contribute to the diagnoses and treatments of different primary physicians
    D. ancillary tests ordered by primary physician to assist in diagnosis and treatment, that do not dominate time and resources

11. The final decision concerning the elimination of an inactive medical record ALWAYS rests with 11.____

    A. the health information manager
    B. medical personnel
    C. the facility's legal counsel
    D. clerical personnel

12. The MOST widely used work quantity monitoring technique in health information departments is 12.____

    A. stopwatch time study
    B. work sampling
    C. direct inspection
    D. employee-reported volume log

13. The GREATEST source of difficulty in the utilization review of a mental health care institution would be 13.____

    A. lack of qualified mental-health personnel to evaluate care for payers
    B. inherent difficulties in evaluating benefit values from claims data
    C. concerns about confidentiality
    D. poor documentation

14. Which of the following risk control techniques is used as a tool to eliminate or reduce future adverse occurrences?

    A. Medical staff minutes
    B. Incident reporting
    C. Occurrence screening
    D. Hazard surveillance

15. The Family Medical Leave Act of 1993 allowing 12 weeks of unpaid leave per year, for specified purposes, applies to all organizations with _____ or more employees.

    A. 10   B. 25   C. 50   D. 100

16. If a court can be assured that a medical record is reliable and trustworthy, the record may be entered into evidence subject to rules relating to all of the following EXCEPT

    A. privilege
    B. adhesion
    C. relevancy
    D. materiality

17. If file cabinets used for storage in a health information department are arranged facing each other, the aisle between cabinets should be _____ wide.

    A. 24 inches
    B. 36 inches
    C. 4 feet
    D. 5 feet

18. The purpose of V codes in the Tabular List of the ICD-9-CM classification system is to code circumstances

    A. particular to obstetric patients and newborns
    B. other than a disease or injury classifiable in the main part of the Tabular List
    C. related to the morphologies and behaviors that are particular to neoplasms
    D. and environmental events as the cause of injury

19. Which of the following data would NOT be a subdivision of clinical data?

    A. Administrative
    B. Ancillary
    C. Medical
    D. Nursing

20. When interviewing an applicant for a position in the department, a _____ question is asked to pose a hypothetical problem.

    A. probing
    B. situational
    C. reflection
    D. clarification

21. When designing a form where data would be entered with a typewriter, how many lines of type should be figured for each vertical inch of space?

    A. 2   B. 4   C. 6   D. 8

22. The GREATEST threat to the confidentiality of health care data is through

    A. re-disclosure by authorized third party
    B. unauthorized disclosure by patients
    C. verbal disclosure of data elements
    D. computerized systems

23. The LEAST productive subject for discussion in a meeting of the health information department would be

    A. deciding which members of the department should take responsibility for specific functions
    B. brainstorming ways to ensure the prompt return of medical records
    C. ensuring the even distribution of filing tasks among clerical personnel
    D. resolution of questions regarding the coding procedure of medical records

24. A _____ would NOT be an effective way to present a frequency distribution.

    A. bar graph
    B. histogram
    C. pie graph
    D. pictogram

25. Which of the following would be considered an ADVANTAGE of using a problem-oriented medical record?

    A. It requires consideration of the context of a patient's complaint.
    B. Its relative simplicity
    C. The maintenance of a chronological sequence
    D. It allows physicians to rely more on records personnel

---

KEY (CORRECT ANSWERS)

1. D		11. C	
2. D		12. D	
3. B		13. C	
4. C		14. B	
5. D		15. C	
6. B		16. B	
7. D		17. D	
8. C		18. B	
9. C		19. A	
10. C		20. B	

21. C
22. A
23. D
24. A
25. A

TEST 3

DIRECTIONS: Each question or incomplete statement is followed by several suggested answers or completions. Select the one that BEST answers the question or completes the statement. *PRINT THE LETTER OF THE CORRECT ANSWER IN THE SPACE AT THE RIGHT.*

1. Which of the following problems would be considered the LEAST serious offense committed by an employee in the department?   1._____

    A. Discourtesy
    B. Absence without notice for three consecutive days
    C. Negligence
    D. Violation of emergency regulations

2. The *work standard* for transcription staff is 20 units per hour with no more than 2 errors per unit. During a given period, employees completed 144 out of 160 expected units, for a backlog of 16 units. Work sampled from one hour of completed work revealed that 16 of 18 units completed did not meet the error standard.
   What is the activity level of the transcription staff?   2._____

    A. 75%   B. 80%   C. 90%   D. 95%

3. What is the productivity level of the transcription staff described in the previous question?   3._____

    A. 75%   B. 80%   C. 90%   D. 95%

4. Which of the following duplicating methods would MOST effectively and economically reproduce the greatest number of forms?   4._____

    A. Photocopying   B. Spirit duplicating
    C. Offset duplicating   D. Stencil duplicating

5. Abstracted case-mix data are used to   5._____

    A. evaluate the quality of care in the facility
    B. accumulate risk management data
    C. determine whether treatment and procedures provided were necessary and appropriate for diagnosis
    D. predict the health care facility's income

6. In determining whether a worker would be defined as *exempt* under the rules of the FLSA (Fair Labor and Standards Act), each of the following factors about the employee should be considered EXCEPT the   6._____

    A. percentage of time spent performing routine, manual, or clerical work
    B. discretionary authority for independent action
    C. earnings level of the employee
    D. overall benefit to the department according to established indexes

7. The 1985 Uniform Health Care Information Act (UHIA) encompasses each of the following principal rules regarding medical information EXCEPT the   7._____

A. provision for patient access to any record
B. provision for the patient to request revision or correction of the record
C. provision for the patient to withhold the content of a medical record even if it is subpoenaed
D. prohibition of provider from disseminating information to a third party without the patient's consent

8. Which of the following incentive pay schemes is currently used by the management in health information departments to guarantee a minimum pay to the employees of a transcription department?

   A. Strict unit-of-measure
   B. Calculated average over a specified time period as the basis for determining an hourly rate
   C. Fixed hourly rate
   D. Premium for units of measure over a minimum

9. In devising a plan for disposing inactive records in a department, one must consider each of the following EXCEPT the

   A. readmission rate for inpatients and outpatients
   B. rate at which potentially compensable events occur in the facility
   C. volume of research
   D. applicable statutes of limitations

10. A statistical analysis of medical record documentation is used PRIMARILY to

    A. identify areas of the record that are incomplete
    B. abstract data to aid clinical or administrative decision-making
    C. identify obvious and routine omissions in the record
    D. identify inconsistent or inaccurate documentation

11. At midnight on April 29, there were 455 patients in a hospital. On April 30, 21 more patients were admitted, and 18 patients either died or were discharged. Three patients were both admitted and discharged on April 30. What was the total number of inpatient service days on April 30?

    A. 458   B. 461   C. 473   D. 476

12. Consultations are *usually* required for treatment for each of the following types of patients EXCEPT patients

    A. whose diagnoses are obscure
    B. who may have been involved in criminal activity
    C. who require cytoscopic procedures
    D. who are not good surgical risks

13. In order to generate current listings, a hospital's computerized R-ADT system links the nursing patient database with the

    A. patient acuity database
    B. personnel database
    C. report generator
    D. automated staff scheduling system

14. A 200-bed community hospital has an average occupancy of 82%. The transcription personnel of the health information department are each assigned a minimum daily product of 1000 words, and the average lines of work produced each month is 160,000. There are 20 workdays in each month.
    Factoring in a 15% adjustment requirement, how many full-time equivalents (FTE's) would be considered a MINIMUM staffing requirement for transcription personnel?

    A. 8   B. 8.8   C. 9.2   D. 10

15. Which of the following is NOT a risk financing fund that would be commonly associated with a facility's risk management program?

    A. Commercial insurance
    B. Insurance pools
    C. Insurance hierarchies
    D. Self-insurance

16. According to the American Health Information Management Association, disease indexes should be retained for AT LEAST

    A. 5 years
    B. 10 years
    C. until the age of the majority, plus the operative statute of limitations
    D. permanently

17. Which of the following risk control techniques is used to identify areas of potential environmental risk prior to an adverse occurrence?

    A. Medical staff minutes
    B. Incident reporting
    C. Occurrence screening
    D. Hazard surveillance

18. Which of the following items would be classified as *ordinal* data for the purpose of research studies?

    A. Low/medium/high values
    B. IQ results
    C. True/false responses
    D. 0-100 scale

19. Which of the following items is NOT currently being released by hospitals as a component of the HCFA Mortality Data?

    A. Percentage of Medicare beneficiaries who die within 30 days of admission
    B. Expected percentage of deaths, calculated on the basis of overall national experience
    C. Percentage of Medicare beneficiaries who die during surgical procedures
    D. Number of Medicare beneficiaries treated

20. According to the GLOSSARY OF HEALTH CARE TERMS, the number of inpatients/residents present at census-taking time each day, plus any inpatients/residents who were both admitted and discharged after the census-taking time the previous day, is known as the

    A. daily census
    B. inpatient/resident service day
    C. census
    D. average daily census

21. Most public health laws require health care institutions to report each of the following diseases or occurrences EXCEPT

    A. births
    B. all tumorous growths
    C. deaths
    D. gunshot wounds

22. NOT a commonly used method of analyzing computerized data systems is

    A. structured analysis
    B. HIPO
    C. network analysis
    D. traditional

23. In a given time period, the distribution of fifteen hospital inpatient stays was as follows: 5, 1, 2, 3, 4, 5, 3, 1, 2, 1, 5, 1, 18, 8, 1. The total of these stays is 60. What would the MEDIAN length of stay for this period be?

    A. 4   B. 3   C. 2   D. 1

24. The Joint Commission's legal standards for the medical record state that the medical record must contain sufficient information for each of the following EXCEPT

    A. requisition for data for research purposes
    B. justification of the treatment
    C. accurate documentation of the course and results
    D. facilitation of continuity of care among providers

25. Which of the following is NOT commonly used to control data misuse in the health information department?

    A. Algorithmic scrambling of all data stored in computer systems
    B. Detailed accounting of computer use
    C. Adoption of log-in procedures
    D. Random monitoring of computer use

KEY (CORRECT ANSWERS)

1. A
2. C
3. B
4. C
5. D

6. D
7. C
8. D
9. B
10. B

11. B
12. C
13. A
14. C
15. C

16. B
17. D
18. A
19. C
20. A

21. B
22. C
23. B
24. A
25. A

EXAMINATION SECTION
TEST 1

DIRECTIONS: Each question or incomplete statement is followed by several suggested answers or completions. Select the one that BEST answers the question or completes the statement. *PRINT THE LETTER OF THE CORRECT ANSWER IN THE SPACE AT THE RIGHT.*

1. All of the following data should be collected for case mix management in a physician's office EXCEPT the

   A. patient's sex
   B. payer mix
   C. patient's race/ethnicity
   D. employment status of patients

   1.____

2. In any edition of the Current Procedural Terminology (CPT) nomenclature system, deleted terms are denoted by

   A. a *0* symbol   B. parentheses
   C. a ^ symbol   D. quotation marks

   2.____

3. Information concerning _____ would NOT be included in the *therapy* plans section of a problem-oriented medical record.

   A. drugs   B. medical procedures
   C. patient education   D. treatment goals

   3.____

4. If a hospital uses a decentralized filing system, *only* the _____ records are stored in a central file.

   A. inpatient   B. outpatient
   C. emergency   D. ancillary

   4.____

5. According to the GLOSSARY OF HEALTH CARE TERMS, which of the following is NOT a commonly used meaning for the word *service*?
   A

   A. group of inpatient beds
   B. division or unit of medical staff responsibility
   C. categorical procedure performed on patients with related diseases
   D. group of discharged patients with related diseases or treatments

   5.____

6. Which of the following is NOT one of the main purposes of a subject/title file in a *paper forms control* program?
   To

   A. record all directives authorizing the use of every form
   B. detect those forms that might be eliminated or consolidated with other forms
   C. avoid the creation of a new form when an existing form could be revised to serve the need
   D. generate studies of forms in relation to the systems and procedures used

   6.____

7. Which of the following is a rule for using the phonetic filing system for a Master Patient Index?

   A. When a repeated key letter or its equivalent is separated by a vowel, treat the two letters as a single unit.
   B. If a name contains more than three key letters, add zeros to arrive at the code number.
   C. If two of the same key letters or a key letter and its equivalent are separated by an *h* or *w*, code two key letters.
   D. When two or more key letters or their equivalents occur together, each letter should be considered separately.

8. Of the following components of a managerial planning function, _____ USUALLY takes the form of annual descriptions of departmental activity.

   A. strategic planning
   B. tactical planning
   C. operational planning
   D. mission

9. Of the following, the MOST serious disadvantage associated with a straight numeric filing system would be the

   A. relatively high probability of misfiling
   B. difficulty of quality control
   C. unequal distribution of filing activity throughout a single department
   D. frequent transposition of numbers

10. The employee privacy rights that are defined in various state laws include each of the following subcategories EXCEPT

    A. rights in workplace investigation
    B. substance abuse and drug testing
    C. polygraph and honesty testing
    D. rights to records

11. The implementation of quality assurance in a mental health care facility requires special adaptations.
    Of the following, which adaptive procedure is MOST characteristic of the review of quality assurance in mental health care facilities?

    A. Involvement of professional staff peer review
    B. Income, outcome indicators being measured incrementally over long periods of time
    C. Clinical performance of individuals without clinical privileges being monitored and evaluated
    D. Relevant findings from the review being used to renew or revise individual clinical privileges

12. A hospital rendered 3,650 inpatient service days in April, a month which has 30 days. What was the average daily inpatient census during Apr

    A. 12   B. 42   C. 122   D. 1,216

13. In nomenclature system categories, the cause of a disease or injury is denoted by the term

    A. etiology
    B. immunology
    C. insertion
    D. origin

14. Of the following management systems, which would be considered the MOST successful model for directing the work of others?

    A. Exploitive-authoritative
    B. Representative
    C. Benevolent-authoritative
    D. Consultative

15. Of the following types of information, _____ is LEAST likely to be included on a graphic sheet.

    A. temperature
    B. fluid output
    C. pulse
    D. respiration

16. Which of the following is NOT an advantage associated with the use of self-contained media (such as endless loop or tanks) for the recording of transcription data?

    A. Strict control of input priorities
    B. Elimination of re-recording necessity
    C. Minimization of lost dictation
    D. Elimination of the physical handling of media

17. Health information data indexes direct the process of locating health information for use by

    A. administration in management and financial decisions
    B. funding agencies or third-party payers for reviewing the necessity for care and its appropriateness
    C. licensing bodies for reviewing the quality of care
    D. physicians in patient care and research

18. Which of the following is considered to be a benefit of a management-by-objective program?

    A. Economic time use
    B. Easily quantifiable results
    C. Reduction of role ambiguity
    D. Reduction in paperwork

19. Of the following, which type of patient death would be included in a hospital's calculation of its mortality rate?

    A. Patients who are dead on arrival
    B. Patients who die while receiving lifesaving services in any unit other than the emergency unit
    C. Patients who die in emergency rooms when no decision has been made about room, board, or nursing service
    D. Fetal deaths

20. A COMMON failure of a management-by-objective program is

    A. the inadequate use of human resources
    B. the inhibitions of the planning function
    C. overemphasis on short-term results
    D. a reduction in managerial motivation

21. Of the following, which incentive pay scheme is MOST often used by health information department management for employees of a transcription department?

    A. Strict unit-of-measure
    B. Calculated average over a specified time period as the basis for determining an hourly rate
    C. Fixed hourly rate
    D. Premium for units of measure over a minimum

22. LEAST likely to be monitored by the utilization review of a hospice record is (are)

    A. appropriateness of admission
    B. stays of fewer than six months
    C. delays in providing team service
    D. appropriateness of the level of service

23. Which of the following is NOT used to measure the central tendency of a grouped set of data?

    A. Mean   B. Median   C. Range   D. Mode

24. The follow-up generation of computerized tumor registries keep track of the status of all registered cancer patients through letters that are generated at intervals of

    A. 6 months   B. 15 months   C. 2 years   D. 30 months

25. Which of the following is NOT one of the main item headings in the Uniform Hospital Discharge Data Set (UHDDS)?

    A. Admission and discharge dates
    B. Diagnoses
    C. Residence
    D. Medical history

KEY (CORRECT ANSWERS)

1. C
2. B
3. C
4. A
5. C

6. A
7. B
8. B
9. C
10. A

11. B
12. C
13. A
14. B
15. B

16. B
17. D
18. C
19. B
20. C

21. B
22. B
23. C
24. B
25. D

TEST 2

DIRECTIONS: Each question or incomplete statement is followed by several suggested answers or completions. Select the one that BEST answers the question or completes the statement. *PRINT THE LETTER OF THE CORRECT ANSWER IN THE SPACE AT THE RIGHT.*

1. Which of the following notations would be considered acceptable, upon being reviewed during a qualitative analysis? 1._____

    A. Patient given instructions
    B. Test results normal
    C. Patient doing well
    D. Watch condition of toes

2. Open-shelf storage units are recommended instead of cabinets for the storage of medical record files for each of the following reasons EXCEPT 2._____

    A. lower cost
    B. faster pulling and filing by personnel
    C. more records can be accommodated in a given floor area
    D. relative neatness

3. To be eligible for FMLA (Family Medical Leave Act) leave, an employee must have worked for an organization for AT LEAST _____ months, not necessarily consecutively. 3._____

    A. 3   B. 9   C. 12   D. 18

4. In nomenclature system categories, the term *function* refers to 4._____

    A. a structural change in tissue
    B. physiological or chemical disorders and alterations resulting from a disease or injury
    C. the part of the body affected by disease or injury
    D. the cause of disease or injury

5. According to the generally accepted legal principle regarding medical records, the physical record is the property of the 5._____

    A. patient   B. payer
    C. provider   D. health care institution

6. The health information practitioner should be concerned about each of the following aspects of data loss EXCEPT 6._____

    A. a contract with a commercial service that spells out terms of protection and remuneration
    B. back-up systems
    C. financial insurance for off-line storage facility damage
    D. monitoring maintenance procedures

7. Which type of HMO is considered to be a discrete organization, possessing its own self-contained records department?

   A. Staff model
   B. Independent practice association
   C. Preferred provider
   D. Group model or closed

8. If a health information department were to switch from serial numbering to unit numbering, which of the following procedures would no longer be performed?

   A. Assigning readmitted patients a new unit number
   B. Cross-referencing empty folders of previous records
   C. Assigning unit numbers to files of patients that have not been readmitted
   D. Leaving empty folders of previous records in their original places in the file

9. In a typical color-coded filing system, two-digit primary numbers from 70-79 would be represented by a band of

   A. purple
   B. brown
   C. red
   D. light green

10. Of the following, _____ is NOT a basic element of a department's revenue and expense budget.

    A. revenues
    B. materials
    C. expenses
    D. personnel

11. Currently, the most advanced administrative computer applications include each of the following areas or departments of health care EXCEPT

    A. laboratory
    B. pharmacy
    C. surgery
    D. dietary

12. When a hospital's medical staff is NOT organized into units, the determining factor for data categorization should be whether

    A. a prescription was ordered by the physician
    B. a surgical operation was performed
    C. ancillary procedures were performed
    D. the patient was an inpatient or outpatient

13. Which of the following types of forms will USUALLY take the longest to reproduce, and therefore require the greatest *lead time* in ordering?

    A. Tags and envelopes
    B. Continuous forms
    C. Carbon-interleaved snapout forms
    D. Single-part forms (larger than 11" x 17")

14. Which element of the paper forms control procedure has been replaced by the *programming logic* element of a computerized environment?

    A. Forms inventory
    B. Forms identification
    C. Ongoing review
    D. Purchasing

15. When medical records are to be microfilmed for storage, the MOST commonly used size of film is _____ mm.

    A. 16　　　B. 35　　　C. 70　　　D. 105

16. In a terminal digit file, the record number 00-00-97 would be followed by the number

    A. 01-00-97　　　B. 00-01-97　　　C. 00-00-98　　　D. 01-01-97

17. The patient summary of a home care patient must be documented and forwarded to the patient's attending physician, and the referral source, AT LEAST once every

    A. 31 days　　　B. 61 days　　　C. 6 months　　　D. year

18. A health information department's work year, minus vacation, sick leave, and holidays, is equal to 47 weeks per year, or 1,880 hours. The department employs two full-time abstracting personnel, who combine to abstract a total of 20,500 records in one year. The time standard for abstracting one record is 10 minutes.
    What is the productivity of the abstracting personnel?

    A. 76%　　　B. 88%　　　C. 91%　　　D. 98%

19. If the personnel described in the previous question improve their production, how many additional records (maximum) could they be expected to abstract in one year, without increasing the required number of full-time employees (FTEs)?

    A. 540　　　B. 1230　　　C. 5400　　　D. 21,730

20. Which of the following would be included in the database section of a problem-oriented medical record?

    A. Social problems　　　B. Systemic review
    C. Specific diagnosis　　　D. Abnormal findings

21. _____ top management plans cover approximately 3-5 years.

    A. Strategic　　　B. Tactical
    C. Operational　　　D. Mission

22. The Privacy Act of 1974 was enacted to protect the privacy of individuals identified in information systems, and gives these individuals access to records concerning themselves, in these systems.
    In the area of health care, this act applies to the medical records of patients

    A. at federal government hospitals *only*
    B. at federal government hospitals and all long-term care facilities
    C. at federal government hospitals and all private inpatient facilities
    D. served by any licensed health care professional

23. If a hospital currently has 50 delinquent records in total, and it averages 75 discharges per completion period, what is the hospital's delinquent record rate?

    A. 25%　　　B. 33%　　　C. 50%　　　D. 67%

24. During insurance audits, which part of the medical record is compared to the services rendered by matching the record item-for-item against the itemized bill?   24.____

   A. Physician's orders
   B. Physical examination
   C. Attestation statement
   D. Discharge record

25. In the standard formula for approximating the size of a research sample, a certainty factor of 97% would be expressed as the number   25.____

   A. 1.281   B. 1.645   C. 1.960   D. 2.170

KEY (CORRECT ANSWERS)

1. D
2. D
3. C
4. B
5. D

6. C
7. A
8. C
9. D
10. B

11. C
12. B
13. B
14. B
15. A

16. A
17. B
18. C
19. B
20. B

21. A
22. A
23. D
24. A
25. D

EXAMINATION SECTION
TEST 1

DIRECTIONS: Each question or incomplete statement is followed by several suggested answers or completions. Select the one that BEST answers the question or completes the statement. *PRINT THE LETTER OF THE CORRECT ANSWER IN THE SPACE AT THE RIGHT.*

1. In residential care facilities, a discharge plan is begun

    A. when news of an impending transfer or referral is received
    B. at the time of admission
    C. when it is clear that the patient will survive treatment
    D. no later than 30 days prior to discharge

2. In hospitals, more statistical data is collected on _____ patients than on any type of patient.

    A. ancillary   B. in-
    C. emergency   D. out-

3. When a phonetic filing system is used for entering data into a Master Patient Index, all names are coded as a

    A. discrete three-letter block
    B. one-syllable surname substitute that excludes vowel sounds
    C. three-digit number
    D. two-digit number preceded by the key consonant in the patient's surname

4. In planning the layout of a health information department, how many square feet of working space should be allowed for each member of the clerical staff?

    A. 10   B. 30   C. 60   D. 120

5. Patient care supplies typically account for about _____ % of a hospital's operating budget.

    A. 10   B. 20   C. 35   D. 50

6. Of the following, an example of a department's risk identification techniques would be

    A. preventive maintenance   B. hazard surveillance
    C. medical staff minutes   D. insurance pools

7. Each of the following is an item in home care records that is *usually* monitored EXCEPT

    A. initial assessments and care plans
    B. documentation of care plan reviews
    C. documentation of all visits
    D. physician's progress notes

8. In a _____ numbering/filing system, the number that the patient receives upon his FIRST visit to a facility is retained for all subsequent visits and treatments.

    A. serial   B. family
    C. unit   D. terminal digit

25

9. Of the following items, the _____ would NOT be a concern of a PRO physician reviewing a hospital's DRG concerns.

   A. selection of principal diagnosis
   B. quality of patient care
   C. substantiation of diagnosis and procedures by the medical record
   D. correct coding of decision tree procedures

10. The edition date of any form should appear next to the

    A. instructions   B. introduction
    C. form number   D. page number

11. When a patient is discharged from a hospital, the source-oriented record is rearranged according to

    A. date, in reverse chronological order in each section
    B. date, from admission to discharge in each section
    C. section, from admission to discharge in each section
    D. section, according to prominence in treatment

12. Which of the following is NOT a filing option used for keeping an incomplete medical record in a health information department?

    A. Permanent file
    B. Separate incomplete file, by provider name
    C. Separate incomplete file, by medical record number
    D. Separate incomplete file, by patient name

13. Coding employees in a health information department are expected to accurately code 7 records of discharged patients in an hour. 20,500 discharges are expected in a year at the hospital. It is assumed that an employee's regular productive time per year is 47 weeks, or 1,880 hours.
    How many full-time equivalents (FTE's) will be required to staff the coding department?

    A. 1.1   B. 1.56   C. 6.4   D. 10.9

14. A quantitative analysis of medical record documentation is used PRIMARILY to

    A. identify areas of the record that are incomplete
    B. abstract data to aid in clinical or administrative decision-making
    C. identify potentially compensable events to be reported to the facility's risk management
    D. identify inconsistent or inaccurate documentation

15. The term used to describe a condition that exists on admission and may increase the length of a patient's stay by at least one day is

    A. accession   B. comorbidity
    C. recurrence   D. complication

16. The MOST frequently used value to express or measure the variation of a set of data is

    A. variance   B. standard deviation
    C. rate   D. range

3 (#1)

17. Of the following components of a managerial planning function, _____ plans are considered to be the MOST specific and verifiable.   17.____

    A. strategic
    B. tactical
    C. operational
    D. mission

18. According to federal regulations, an Annual Reporting Form must be filed with the EEOC by all employers with _____ or more employees.   18.____

    A. 50   B. 100   C. 200   D. 500

19. Which of the following is a binary data representation of the number 13?   19.____

    A. 0111   B. 1101   C. 0001   D. 101

20. A health information department's annual budget for supply expenditures is $7,000. Nine months into the year, the department has spent a total of $5,400 on supplies.   20.____
    The projection calculation for the department's year-end total expenditures should be _____ budget.

    A. $150 under   B. $100 under   C. $150 over   D. $200 over

21. Of the following commonly recognized management functions, which function would be considered to be the *feedback* mechanism?   21.____

    A. Controlling
    B. Directing
    C. Planning
    D. Organizing

22. Typically, the fine imposed on a health insurance facility which violates regulations concerning the privacy of medical records more than once would not exceed   22.____

    A. $500   B. $1500   C. $5000   D. $25,000

23. Which of the following is considered to be an ADVANTAGE associated with the use of a source-oriented medical record?   23.____

    A. Ease in determining the assessments and treatments of particular departments
    B. The clear indication of goals and methods in patient treatment
    C. That it requires consideration of the context of a patient's complaint
    D. That it allows physicians to rely more on records personnel

24. Problems with the use of integrated medical records are MOST frequently associated with   24.____

    A. medical histories
    B. physician's orders
    C. progress notes
    D. consultation reports

25. In any research study, which of the following steps would occur FIRST?   25.____

    A. Pilot study is conducted
    B. Research design is selected
    C. Research hypothesis is stated
    D. Data gathering instruments and procedures are developed

KEY (CORRECT ANSWERS)

1. B
2. B
3. C
4. C
5. B

6. C
7. D
8. C
9. B
10. C

11. B
12. D
13. B
14. A
15. B

16. B
17. C
18. B
19. B
20. D

21. A
22. C
23. A
24. C
25. B

TEST 2

DIRECTIONS: Each question or incomplete statement is followed by several suggested answers or completions. Select the one that BEST answers the question or completes the statement. *PRINT THE LETTER OF THE CORRECT ANSWER IN THE SPACE AT THE RIGHT.*

1. In a residential or long-term care psychiatric facility, a patient's records should be reviewed

    A. daily B. weekly C. monthly D. annually

2. Which of the following functions in the management of a health care information department is LEAST likely to be facilitated by commercial software packages?

    A. Budgeting
    B. Utilization review
    C. Staff scheduling
    D. Statistical calculations

3. Each of the following is a basic element of a nursing department's computerized administrative information system EXCEPT the

    A. report generator
    B. automated scheduling system
    C. automated acuity system
    D. medication administration system

4. In order to plan an operating expense budget, each of the following must be known EXCEPT the

    A. unit of service activity
    B. unit cost
    C. work distribution
    D. expense type

5. A health information department currently using 1,435 linear filing inches to store records intends to replace its open-shelf filing units. Each of the shelves in a new five-shelf unit measures 33 linear filing inches.
It is estimated that an additional 300 filing inches should be added to allow for five-year expansion capabilities. How many shelving units should be purchased?

    A. 7 B. 10 C. 11 D. 13

6. In the *Reason for Encounter* classification system, each item is coded as a

    A. letter followed by two digits
    B. digit followed by two letters
    C. two-digit number with one decimal digit subcategory
    D. three-digit number

7. According to the World Health Organization's definitions for reporting reproductive health statistics, any neonate whose birth occurs from the first day (267th day) of the 39th week, through the end of the last day of the 42nd week (294th day) following the onset of the last menstrual period, would be termed _____ neonate.

    A. low birthweight
    B. preterm
    C. term
    D. post-term

8. Medicare's UB-92 form for billing data includes space for _____ procedure code(s).

   A. 1   B. 3   C. 6   D. 9

9. Of the following devices, the _____ is commonly used in health information departments to graphically display a specific project's time line and progress.

   A. bar graph
   B. Gantt chart
   C. line graph
   D. histogram

10. Which component of the cancer registry contains the abstracts of cancer patients who received all or part of their FIRST course of treatment at the reporting facility?

    A. Case files
    B. Master index file
    C. Accession register
    D. Follow-up file

11. The _____ technique used by health information management to monitor the *quality* of work is patterned after the production industry.

    A. questionnaire
    B. checklist
    C. report
    D. audit

12. The health information practitioner is *usually* responsible for working with the chair of the record committee to prepare the agenda for committee meetings which must be held AT LEAST

    A. monthly
    B. quarterly
    C. biannually
    D. annually

13. When a patient is admitted to a hospital, a medical history will NOT be required if a previous, unaltered history has been performed no more than _____ prior to the patient's admission.

    A. two weeks
    B. thirty days
    C. six months
    D. one year

14. Of the following types of medical record delinquencies, a missing _____ would be considered LEAST serious.

    A. discharge summary
    B. medical history report
    C. signature on attestation
    D. operative report

15. If a home care patient were to require eight or more hours of daily nursing care, which of the Medicare reimbursement categories would be imposed?

    A. Continuous home care
    B. Routine home care
    C. General inpatient care
    D. Inpatient respite care

16. A quantitative analysis of medical record documentation includes, as a basic requirement, a review of the record for

    A. a recording of all necessary instances of informed consent
    B. a consistent recording of diagnostic statements
    C. the required authentication on all entries
    D. the description and justification of the course of a patient's hospitalization

17. The ideal number of digits in a record number is

    A. 4   B. 5   C. 6   D. 7

18. Which type of HMO follows the same type of record-keeping practices as the independent practice association?

    A. Group model or closed
    B. Staff model
    C. Multi-specialty
    D. Preferred provider

19. Of the following, _____ plans would be considered to be the driving force behind management's planning function.

    A. strategic
    B. tactical
    C. operational
    D. mission

20. When reviewing a medical record for entry consistency, health information professionals should seek entries that could result in the miscommunication of patient care information.
    Each of the following is a common source of this type of miscommunication EXCEPT

    A. progress notes written by different members of a health care team
    B. admission record data recorded by more than one member of a health care team
    C. mismatched orders and medication records
    D. admission and discharge information recorded by different health care personnel

21. A quantitative analysis of medical record documentation is LEAST likely to be useful in solving problems associated with

    A. dating of entries
    B. illegibility or incomplete content
    C. inappropriate correction of errors
    D. spaces that should be lined through to prevent tampering

22. When a health care institution is required by public health laws to report certain diseases or occurrences, the responsibility for reporting USUALLY rests with the

    A. provider
    B. health information department
    C. admissions department
    D. payer

23. An *encounter,* according to standard ambulatory health care data practices, is defined as a

    A. patient receiving laboratory services through a separate provider after the original encounter
    B. outpatient visiting both a physician's office and a clinic as parts of an individual treatment plan
    C. patient's imaging reports being interpreted, when the patient is not physically present, by someone other than the referring physician
    D. patient receiving services from a pharmacist

24. When an applicant is being interviewed for a position in the department, the rules of the EEOC would permit questions about the applicant's

    A. spouse's occupation
    B. convictions for criminal activity
    C. military record
    D. plans for beginning a family

25. The _____ would typically be included in the admitting evaluation or assessment of a patient in a long-term care facility.

    A. stop orders for medications
    B. after-care recommendations
    C. social history
    D. name of the transferring or referring institution

KEY (CORRECT ANSWERS)

1. C	11. D
2. B	12. B
3. D	13. B
4. C	14. A
5. C	15. A
6. A	16. C
7. C	17. C
8. C	18. A
9. B	19. D
10. A	20. B

21. B
22. A
23. A
24. B
25. C

EXAMINATION SECTION
TEST 1

DIRECTIONS: Each question or incomplete statement is followed by several suggested answers or completions. Select the one that BEST answers the question or completes the statement. *PRINT THE LETTER OF THE CORRECT ANSWER IN THE SPACE AT THE RIGHT.*

1. Which of the following would be included in the problem list section of a problem-oriented medical record?

    A. Medical history
    B. Patient profile
    C. Statement of symptom
    D. Baseline laboratory data

2. A summary list that is required documentation for each patient in a free-standing ambulatory care facility should

    A. include a catalog of all medications taken
    B. not repeat recurring problems or diagnoses
    C. include a long-term diagnosis based on the summary list itself
    D. include the date of each patient visit

3. Each of the following is *usually* included in the transfer/referral form for patients in long-term care facilities EXCEPT the

    A. time period for which care is anticipated
    B. estimate of rehabilitative potential
    C. physical examination
    D. level of care required

4. When medical records are to be microfilmed for storage, how many letter-sized images can be transferred onto a 100-foot roll of the most commonly used microfilm?

    A. 1600   B. 2500   C. 4500   D. 6000

5. When using a phonetic filing system for entering data into a Master Patient Index, the name *Martin* would be coded

    A. 563   B. 635   C. 565   D. 656

6. A hospital has an inpatient bed count of 150 during June, which has 30 days. During June, the hospital rendered 3,650 service days to inpatients.
What was the hospital's inpatient bed occupancy rate for June?

    A. 8%   B. 24%   C. 56%   D. 81%

7. Which of the following is a MINIMUM requirement for inclusion in a patient's mental health record?

    A. Description of any functional limitations
    B. Orders authenticated by patient's physician
    C. Individualized aftercare or post treatment plan
    D. Name of the patient's physician

8. In nomenclature system categories, a structural change in tissue is denoted by the term

   A. etiology
   B. fracture
   C. topography
   D. morphology

9. Each of the following is a *minimum* data requirement for a cancer registry's master index file EXCEPT

   A. patient's race/ethnicity
   B. social security number
   C. accession number
   D. patient's age at diagnosis

10. Which of the following data control procedures reviews the quality of outputs from a data system and the adequacy of quality control for these systems?

    A. Specifying standards
    B. Abstract review
    C. Quality control
    D. Audit

11. At midnight on April 29, there are 455 patients in a hospital. On April 30, 21 more patients are admitted, and 18 patients either died or were discharged. 3 patients were both admitted and discharged on April 30. What was the inpatient census at midnight on April 30?

    A. 458
    B. 461
    C. 473
    D. 476

12. A problem-oriented record includes all of the following categories EXCEPT

    A. therapy
    B. diagnosis and management
    C. contingency plans
    D. patient education

13. A secondary condition that arises during hospitalization and is thought to increase the length of a patient's stay by at least one day, is termed

    A. accession
    B. comorbidity
    C. recurrence
    D. complication

14. In the ICD-Oncology classification system, the morphology and behavior of a neoplasm is coded as a

    A. series of paired letters
    B. pair of letters linked with a two-digit number
    C. four-digit number
    D. five-digit number

15. Which of the following is NOT one of the major usage applications for computers in health care?

    A. Financial
    B. Research
    C. Administrative
    D. Clinical

16. When a graph is used to present data with an upper-level frequency spread, the term for the device used to omit the zero line is

    A. lightning mark
    B. squelch
    C. carat
    D. dependent variable mark

17. Which of the following is NOT an advantage associated with the use of a problem-oriented medical record?

   A. Facilitation of quality assurance procedures
   B. Clear indication of goals and methods in patient treatment
   C. Consolidation of information concerning a particular episode of care
   D. Facilitation of medical education

17.____

18. A statement of goals for resident patient treatment is USUALLY included in the

   A. admitting evaluation
   B. comprehensive care plan
   C. progress notes
   D. physician's orders

18.____

19. Which of the following is NOT an input device for a computer system?

   A. Voice recognition devices
   B. Terminal
   C. CRT screen
   D. Bar code reader

19.____

20. Which volume of the ICD-9-CM is unique among ICD classification systems?

   A. Tabular List
   B. Oncology Index
   C. Procedures
   D. Alphabetical Index

20.____

21. The *median* would be used to calculate the central tendency of a data set in order to

   A. discover the most frequent value in a set
   B. account for an extraordinarily narrow range of values
   C. prevent extreme figures from presenting a misleading interpretation
   D. use a geometric, rather than arithmetic, method of discovering the central tendency

21.____

22. In nomenclature system categories, the term *topography* refers to

   A. a structural change in tissue
   B. physiological or chemical disorders and alterations resulting from a disease or injury
   C. the part of the body affected by disease or injury
   D. the cause of disease or injury

22.____

23. According to standard ambulatory health care data practices, a *professional contact* is defined as

   A. any face-to-face meeting between a patient and a provider
   B. a face-to-face contact between a patient and a provider who has primary assessment and treatment responsibilities for the patient
   C. a specific identifiable instance of an act of service involved in the care of a patient
   D. the visit of a patient to one or more units or facilities located in or directed by the entity that maintains the outpatient care services

23.____

24. Which of the following is NOT one of the minimally required items for a patient index card that is to be filed in the Master Patient Index?

    A. Patient social security number
    B. Identifying number
    C. Patient address
    D. Sex of patient

25. According to the GLOSSARY OF HEALTH CARE TERMS, the number of inpatients/residents present at any one time in a health care facility is known as the

    A. daily census
    B. inpatient/resident service day
    C. census
    D. average daily census

KEY (CORRECT ANSWERS)

1. C	11. A
2. B	12. C
3. C	13. D
4. B	14. D
5. B	15. B
6. D	16. A
7. C	17. C
8. D	18. B
9. B	19. C
10. D	20. C

21. C
22. C
23. B
24. D
25. C

TEST 2

DIRECTIONS: Each question or incomplete statement is followed by several suggested answers or completions. Select the one that BEST answers the question or completes the statement. *PRINT THE LETTER OF THE CORRECT ANSWER IN THE SPACE AT THE RIGHT.*

1. Several copies of a form that are prefastened, collated, and held together by gluing an edge are known as a _____ set. 1.____

    A. form   B. unit   C. stub   D. snapout

2. Each of the following is an item that is routinely entered into the disease/procedure index EXCEPT the 2.____

    A. patient's sex
    B. end results of hospitalization
    C. patient's social security number
    D. patient's race/ethnicity

3. Which of the following is NOT an advantage associated with the use of discrete media (such as cassettes, belts, and disks) for the recording of transcription data? 3.____

    A. A visually measurable end
    B. Ease in counting
    C. Lowered supply/ordering concerns
    D. Quick distribution potential

4. Which type of classification system's manual coding is done through the use of *decision trees*? 4.____

    A. ICD-9-CM   B. DRG   C. RUG   D. APG

5. According to the World Health Organization's definitions for reporting reproductive health statistics, any neonate whose birth occurs before the end of the last day of the 38th week (266th day) following the onset of the last menstrual period is defined as a _____ neonate. 5.____

    A. low birthweight
    B. preterm
    C. term
    D. post-term

6. Which of the following is NOT a module of the Reason for Visit classification system's Tabular List? 6.____

    A. Administrative
    B. Treatment
    C. Diagnoses, diseases
    D. Symptoms

7. An operating room register should be preserved for a MINIMUM period of 7.____

    A. 1 year
    B. 5 years
    C. 10 years
    D. permanently

8. According to the American Health Information Management Association, adult patient health records should be retained for a MINIMUM of 8.____

    A. 5 years
    B. 10 years after the most recent encounter
    C. the age of the majority, plus the operative statute of limitations
    D. permanently

9. Which of the following is NOT typically considered to be a *primary* function of a computerized transcription management system in the health information department?

   A. Facilitation of transcriptionist work assignments
   B. Provision of recommendations for improved work flow
   C. Provision of information on priority jobs and backlogs
   D. Making data available on system activity by physicians

10. Computerized record location/tracking systems in a medical record department USUALLY use _____ as an input device.

    A. keyboarding
    B. bar codes
    C. optical scanners
    D. OCR devices

11. In the event that a patient wants to correct an entry in the medical record, it should be done

    A. over complete erasure of the contested entry
    B. as a separate preface to the entire record, with a line drawn through the contested entry
    C. on a separate form that will be attached to the back of the record, with a referral notation assigned to the contested entry
    D. as an amendment to the original entry, without changing the original

12. After a patient has been discharged from a hospital, the patient's medical record is required to be completed within

    A. 24 hours   B. 48 hours   C. 1 week   D. 30 days

13. Each of the following items is a *minimum* data requirement for a provider's credentials file EXCEPT

    A. education
    B. denial of medical staff privileges at other institutions
    C. initial date of licensure
    D. narcotics number

14. Physical examinations for patients should be repeated

    A. monthly   B. quarterly   C. biannually   D. annually

15. Which of the following types of record-keeping systems is considered LEAST favorable for use in a mental health institution?

    A. Source-oriented
    B. Problem-oriented
    C. Goal-oriented
    D. Integrated

16. Assuming that a quantitative analysis has already been performed, a qualitative analysis of medical record documentation includes, as a basic requirement, a review of the record for

    A. correct patient identification on every form
    B. presence of all necessary reports
    C. consistency in entries by all health care practitioners
    D. required authentication on all entries

17. In a vertical card file, form headers should appear at the

   A. top right
   B. top left
   C. top center
   D. bottom

18. In the _____ numbering/filing system, an outguide typically takes the form of an empty chart folder marked with a number referral.

   A. serial
   B. serial-unit
   C. unit
   D. middle-digit

19. Each of the following is a *case-mix* classification system EXCEPT

   A. RUG   B. DRG   C. ICD   D. APG

20. In a given time period, the distribution of fifteen of a hospital's inpatient stays was as follows: 5, 1, 2, 3, 4, 5, 3, 1, 2, 1, 5, 1, 18, 8, 1. The total of these stays is 60 days. What is the mode length of stay for this period?

   A. 4   B. 3   C. 2   D. 1

21. Which of the following is a binary data representation of the number 10?

   A. 1   B. 11   C. 110   D. 1010

22. A medical transcriptionist using a word processor typically works under a MINIMUM daily product target of _____ words.

   A. 350-750
   B. 800-1000
   C. 1000-1500
   D. 1600-2400

23. The most widely-used ambulatory medical record system, the COSTAR, includes each of the following modules EXCEPT

   A. appointment
   B. medical record
   C. scheduling
   D. management reporting

24. Medicare and Medicaid regulations are found in Title _____ of the Code of Federal Regulations.

   A. 9   B. 14   C. 34   D. 42

25. In 1985, the Joint Commission developed a 10-step process for the quality evaluation of health care facilities.
Which of these steps should be performed FIRST by a quality assurance team?

   A. Identify indicators and criteria
   B. Delineate scope of care
   C. Establish thresholds for evaluation
   D. Collect and organize data

KEY (CORRECT ANSWERS)

1. B
2. C
3. C
4. B
5. B

6. C
7. C
8. B
9. B
10. B

11. D
12. D
13. C
14. D
15. A

16. C
17. D
18. B
19. C
20. D

21. D
22. C
23. A
24. D
25. B

EXAMINATION SECTION
TEST 1

DIRECTIONS: Each question or incomplete statement is followed by several suggested answers or completions. Select the one that BEST answers the question or completes the statement. *PRINT THE LETTER OF THE CORRECT ANSWER IN THE SPACE AT THE RIGHT.*

1. Which of the following is NOT considered to be one of the four *primary* components of departmental management?

    A. Performance
    B. Functions
    C. Objectives
    D. Resources

2. According to the American Health Information Management Association, fetal heart monitor records should be retained for a MINIMUM of

    A. 5 years after the infant reaches the age of the majority
    B. 10 years after the infant reaches the age of the majority
    C. the age of the majority, plus the operative statute of limitations
    D. permanently

3. A hospital medical record is USUALLY

    A. integrated
    B. problem-oriented
    C. source-oriented
    D. computerized

4. Which of the following forms are customarily used in ambulatory care facilities to collect data for billing purposes?

    A. Admission sheets
    B. Encounter forms
    C. Attestation statements
    D. Discharge summaries

5. When medical records are to be microfilmed for storage, the rate of reduction MOST commonly used is

    A. 1/16   B. 1/24   C. 1/50   D. 1/98

6. Which of the following is NOT a disadvantage associated with the use of middle digit filing applications?

    A. Extensive personnel training requirements
    B. Difficulty in handling numbers with seven or more digits
    C. Uneven distribution of record filing requirements
    D. Tendency for large gaps to be created in files

7. Of the following, _____ is NOT an advantage associated with the use of terminal digit filing applications.

    A. reduction in the number of misfiles
    B. fewer shelving/storage units required
    C. reduction in large record gaps that require back-shifting
    D. even distribution of filing load

8. According to the Joint Commission's standards for home health care documentation, which of the following items is NOT a minimal requirement for the home care medical record?

    A. Any instructions given to the patient on discharge by the health care organization
    B. Summaries or copies of records from the transferring organization, if any
    C. Name of the patient's physician
    D. Description of any safety measures needed to protect the patient

9. Which of the following is a *horizontal* component of work allocation?

    A. Span of control
    B. Departmentalization
    C. Delegation
    D. Authority

10. Of the following items in a long-term care patient's identification data, _____ should be included in a highly visible place, in order to be kept current with the resident's clinical record.

    A. marital status
    B. date of admission
    C. insurance
    D. age

11. Which of the following is NOT a type of cancer registry?

    A. Hospital-based
    B. Central registry
    C. Outpatient registry
    D. Special-purpose registry

12. Data which are abstracted from medical records must accurately reflect the original data in each record from which the data was taken.
    This is a standard of the data's

    A. reliability
    B. completeness
    C. validity
    D. accountability

13. Which of the following forms often makes use of margins and columns to allow for the distinction between information supplied by the physician, and information supplied by other personnel?

    A. Pathology reports
    B. Consultation report
    C. Physical examination
    D. Progress notes

14. In a long-term care facility, progress notes should be made by the physician every time

    A. orders are given
    B. a patient is seen
    C. a visit results in quantifiable data
    D. a visit results in physician's orders

15. *Rule-out* statements on a problem-oriented medical record appear in the plans section for

    A. therapy
    B. diagnosis and management
    C. contingency plans
    D. patient education

16. The evaluation and management codes of the Current Procedural Terminology (CPT) nomenclature system take into consideration each of the following EXCEPT

    A. level of medical decision-making required
    B. whether the patient is new or established
    C. extent of history and physical taken
    D. whether the patient is enrolled in an HMO

17. It is necessary to leave about 25% of filing space open to allow for expansion in the _____ numbering/filing system.

    A. serial
    B. serial-unit
    C. unit
    D. family

18. Of the following characteristics of a health care record, _____ would usually NOT be analyzed qualitatively.

    A. use of approved abbreviations
    B. unexplained time gaps
    C. lines drawn through incorrect information
    D. avoidance of extraneous remarks

19. When grouping abstracted data onto a frequency distribution table, the general rule is NOT to group the data into more than _____ classes.

    A. 3   B. 5   C. 10   D. 15

20. According to the American Health Information Management Association, the health records of minors should be retained for a MINIMUM of

    A. 5 years
    B. 10 years
    C. the age of the majority, plus the operative statute of limitations
    D. permanently

21. Which of the following is an example of a risk control technique that would be associated with a risk management program?

    A. Claims management
    B. Results of QI activities
    C. Commercial insurance
    D. Incident report

22. When medical records are to be microfilmed for storage, the _____ numbering/filing system would be the MOST effective application for roll microfilming.

    A. serial
    B. serial-unit
    C. unit
    D. terminal digit

23. During July, 42 inpatient deaths occurred at a hospital. Among these were 4 deaths that had to be reported to the medical examiner. 2 of these 4 bodies were removed from the hospital, and no hospital autopsy was performed. Hospital autopsies were performed on the other two cases. Twelve other autopsies were performed following inpatient deaths during the month.
    What was the net autopsy rate for the hospital in July?

    A. 28%   B. 33%   C. 35%   D. 42%

24. In a typical color-coded filing system, two-digit primary numbers from 40-49 would be represented by a band of

    A. yellow
    B. light blue
    C. red
    D. dark green

25. Which of the following is NOT one of the sections included in the main body of the Current Procedural Terminology (CPT) nomenclature system?

    A. Disbursement options
    B. Medicine
    C. Pathology/laboratory
    D. Radiology

KEY (CORRECT ANSWERS)

1. A		11. C	
2. B		12. C	
3. C		13. D	
4. B		14. B	
5. B		15. B	
6. C		16. D	
7. B		17. C	
8. C		18. C	
9. B		19. D	
10. D		20. C	

21. A
22. A
23. C
24. B
25. A

TEST 2

DIRECTIONS: Each question or incomplete statement is followed by several suggested answers or completions. Select the one that BEST answers the question or completes the statement. *PRINT THE LETTER OF THE CORRECT ANSWER IN THE SPACE AT THE RIGHT.*

1. The MOST common type of imaging report found in medical records is   1.____

    A. MRI   B. xerograph   C. EKG   D. x-ray

2. Which of the following is NOT a specific type of entry that appears in the alphabetical index of the Current Procedural Terminology (CPT) nomenclature system?   2.____

    A. Organ or other anatomic site
    B. Indications
    C. Abbreviations
    D. Procedure or service

3. The MINIMUM amount of space allowable for the bottom margin of any medical record form is _____ inch.   3.____

    A. 1/8   B. 1/4   C. 2/5   D. 1/2

4. The Joint Commission requires the treatment plan for a mental health patient to be reviewed at each of the following key decision points EXCEPT   4.____

    A. at the time of transfer or discharge
    B. every month of inpatient treatment
    C. at the conclusion of initial treatment
    D. every ten visits or three months of outpatient care, whichever comes first

5. The employee rights that are associated with the employment agreement in various state laws include each of the following subcategories EXCEPT   5.____

    A. implied employment contracts
    B. employee free speech
    C. employment at will
    D. due process

6. Source-oriented records are arranged according to   6.____

    A. date, in reverse chronological order in each section
    B. date, from admission to discharge in each section
    C. section, from admission to discharge in each section
    D. section, according to prominence in treatment

7. In a family numbering system for filing medical records, a head of household would be denoted by the number   7.____

    A. 01-123456   B. 06-654321   C. 12-123456   D. 123456-01

8. In any edition of the Current Procedural Terminology (CPT) nomenclature system, revised terms are denoted by   8.____

    A. a *0* symbol   B. parentheses
    C. a ∧ symbol   D. quotation marks

45

9. When a patient's problem is resolved, it should be _____ from the problem list _____, on a problem-oriented record.

   A. marked *dropped;* with a corresponding date
   B. erased; to make room for other entries
   C. marked *N/A;* with a corresponding date
   D. deleted; and added to the progress notes

10. For proper authentication in hospitals with house staff, the attending physician must countersign AT LEAST the medical history, physical examination, and

    A. progress notes
    B. imaging reports
    C. discharge summary
    D. pathology reports

11. The MINIMUM amount of space allowable for the top margin of any medical record form is _____ inch.

    A. 1/16 B. 2/16 C. 1/4 D. 3/8

12. Medicare's UB-92 form for billing data includes space for _____ diagnosis code(s).

    A. 1 B. 3 C. 6 D. 9

13. In the ICD-Oncology classification system, the topography of a neoplasm is coded as a

    A. series of paired letters
    B. pair of letters linked with a two-digit number
    C. four-digit number
    D. five-digit number

14. Each of the following is a basic part of the problem-oriented medical record EXCEPT the

    A. problem list
    B. consultation report
    C. database
    D. progress notes

15. In a serial numbered file, the record number 00-00-97 would be followed by the number

    A. 01-00-97 B. 00-01-97 C. 00-00-98 D. 01-01-97

16. The purpose of a *tickler* file in resident care facilities is to

    A. serve as a substitute for a discharge summary
    B. remind personnel of examinations or treatment updates that are due
    C. provide data that can safely be substituted on updated physical examination forms
    D. remind personnel of their daily progress note requirements

17. Which of the following would be included in the progress notes of a problem-oriented medical record?

    A. Social data
    B. Chief complaint
    C. Plan statements
    D. Medical diagnosis

18. In any edition of the Current Procedural Terminology (CPT) nomenclature system, new terms are denoted by

    A. a *0* symbol
    B. parentheses
    C. a ∧ symbol
    D. quotation marks

19. Legal aspects of the medical record are commonly decided by established precedent, or   19.____

   A. *duces tecum* B. *appurtenance*
   C. *vis major*   D. *stare decisis*

20. Which of the following classification systems is used almost exclusively in radiology departments?   20.____

   A. ICHPPC   B. RFEC   C. Roentgen   D. RVS

21. The preliminary treatment plan for a patient at a mental health institution should be developed within _____ hours of the patient's admission, based upon the assessments conducted within that time frame.   21.____

   A. 24   B. 48   C. 60   D. 72

22. Which of the following is a chronological list of all patient visits?   22.____

   A. Number index   B. Admission register
   C. Cancer registry   D. Master patient index

23. Of the following, _____ is NOT considered to be one of the key considerations for implementing a computer-based record system in an ambulatory care facility.   23.____

   A. the type of patients to be included in the system
   B. whether the system is meant to serve the provider, administration, or research
   C. similarities to the COSTAR system
   D. the structure of data in the record

24. Which of the following is NOT usually a part of a health information practitioner's responsibility in interaction with the medical staff?   24.____

   A. Administering uniform policies for completion of records
   B. Supplying subjective written commentary on a physician's performance
   C. Keeping physicians informed of the number of records requiring completion
   D. Providing statistics on an individual physician's performance

25. Of the following, a _____ file is NOT usually found in a computerized dietary system database.   25.____

   A. food item   B. patient information
   C. staff scheduling D. recipe

KEY (CORRECT ANSWERS)

1. D
2. B
3. D
4. B
5. B

6. A
7. A
8. C
9. A
10. C

11. B
12. D
13. C
14. B
15. C

16. B
17. C
18. A
19. D
20. C

21. D
22. B
23. C
24. B
25. C

EXAMINATION SECTION
TEST 1

DIRECTIONS: Each question or incomplete statement is followed by several suggested answers or completions. Select the one that BEST answers the question or completes the statement. *PRINT THE LETTER OF THE COREECT ANSWER IN THE SPACE AT THE RIGHT.*

1. Each of the following is an administrative form EXCEPT

    A. identification sheet
    B. medical history
    C. summary report
    D. face sheet

    1.____

2. According to Medicare's Conditions for Participation, an emergency care record MUST contain each of the following data elements EXCEPT

    A. history of disease or injury
    B. disposition of the case
    C. statistical abstracts for quality assessment
    D. pertinent laboratory or imaging reports

    2.____

3. In a terminal digit filing system application of the family number 02-623472, the PRIMARY digits are

    A. 02
    B. 62
    C. 34
    D. 72

    3.____

4. Of the following, the _____ index is a confidential record.

    A. physician's
    B. operation
    C. disease/procedure
    D. master patient

    4.____

5. Of the following Medicare reimbursement categories, _____ care is imposed when a home care patient requires acute symptom management that cannot be performed at home.

    A. continuous home
    B. routine home
    C. general inpatient
    D. inpatient respite

    5.____

6. Which of the following is NOT a *minimum* requirement to be included on a patient's written authorization for release of a medical record to a third party?

    A. Inclusive dates of treatment
    B. Name of physician(s) or provider(s) responsible for treatment during inclusive dates
    C. Patient's address
    D. Condition on which the release authorization will expire

    6.____

7. When abstracted from the record of nursing facilities, each of the following statistics has been found useful for management purposes EXCEPT

    A. inpatient census
    B. percentage of occupancy
    C. prior acute care patterns
    D. death rate

    7.____

49

8. In the Tabular List of the ICD-9-CM classification system, a single disease entity is coded as a(n)

    A. alphabetical chain of five letters
    B. letter followed by a four-digit number
    C. three-digit number, with decimal digit subcategories
    D. five-digit number

9. If a medical record is subpoenaed, the standard practice is NOT to remove _____ unless the subpoena specifically calls for such documents.

    A. all correspondence
    B. attestation statements
    C. duplicate copies of reports
    D. insurance reports

10. If a patient is admitted to a facility on June 27 and discharged on July 3, the patient's length of stay is calculated as _____ days.

    A. 5   B. 6   C. 7   D. 8

11. It is NOT a purpose of the quantitative analysis of medical record documentation to

    A. meet licensing requirements
    B. make the record more useful for continuing patient care
    C. assist in diagnosis and procedure-coding specificity
    D. protect the legal interests of the patient

12. Of the following data control procedures, _____ is the basis for measuring conformity to characteristics of excellence, reliability, security, etc.

    A. specifying standards   B. abstract review
    C. quality control   D. audit

13. Which of the following types of facilities are NOT bound by the federal regulation of medical data compiled on drug and alcohol abuse patients?

    A. General medical care facilities with an identified unit set aside for treatment of drug or alcohol abuse patients
    B. Federally-assisted alcohol or drug abuse programs
    C. General hospitals who treat drug or alcohol abuse patients for any reason
    D. All of the above are subject to federal regulations

14. The user should be able to immediately determine each of the following from the title and instructions of any form EXCEPT

    A. how many copies are required
    B. to whom copies should be sent
    C. who should submit the form
    D. who should complete the form

15. According to the alphabetical filing guidelines for entering data into the Master Patient Index, which of the following names would appear FIRST in the Index?

    A. Meredith Brown   B. M. Kay Brown
    C. Mary Kay Brown   D. M. Brown

16. Each of the following is a clinical form EXCEPT

    A. imaging report
    B. physician's orders
    C. progress notes
    D. admission/discharge record

17. According to the Uniform Hospital Discharge Data Set (UHDDS), each of the following would be defined as a *significant procedure* EXCEPT one that

    A. carries an anesthetic risk
    B. requires a prescription
    C. is surgical in nature
    D. requires specialized training

18. Which of the following is an example of a *primary* record?

    A. Medical histories
    B. Indexes containing medical information
    C. Merged clinical and financial data
    D. Quality assurance reports

19. The _____ numbering/filing system requires a patient to receive a new number for each occasion of treatment.

    A. serial   B. serial-unit
    C. unit   D. family

20. According to the Joint Commission's standards for home health care documentation, which of the following items is a MINIMAL requirement for the home care medical record?

    A. A description of any of the patient's functional limitations
    B. Principal and secondary diagnoses on admission
    C. Current medication profile
    D. Notes on the adaptability of the home for health care

21. Of the following words, _____ should NOT be used in a medical history, EXCEPT in summarizing previously stated facts.

    A. aseptic   B. rupture   C. positive   D. normal

22. Which component of the cancer registry contains a chronological list of ALL cancer cases at the reporting facility?

    A. Case files   B. Master index file
    C. Accession register   D. Follow-up file

23. When using a terminal digit system of filing, a clerk would consider the _____ digits to be the *primary* digits of the record number.

    A. first two   B. last two
    C. middle two   D. outer right and left

24. Which of the following is a work quality monitoring technique used by health information department management? 24._____

    A. Stopwatch time study
    B. Work sampling
    C. Direct inspection
    D. Employee-reported volume log

25. In designing a form where data would be entered by hand, how much vertical spacing should be allowed per line? _____ inch. 25._____

    A. 1/16   B. 1/8   C. 1/4   D. 1/2

KEY (CORRECT ANSWERS)

1. B
2. C
3. D
4. A
5. C

6. B
7. C
8. C
9. B
10. B

11. C
12. A
13. C
14. D
15. D

16. D
17. B
18. A
19. A
20. D

21. D
22. C
23. B
24. C
25. C

TEST 2

DIRECTIONS: Each question or incomplete statement is followed by several suggested answers or completions. Select the one that BEST answers the question or completes the statement. *PRINT THE LETTER OF THE CORRECT ANSWER IN THE SPACE AT THE RIGHT.*

1. In figuring a population's infection rate, what term is used for the ratio of known cases of a chronic disease at any given point in time to the population at that time? 1.____

    A. Incidence
    B. Etiology
    C. Morbidity
    D. Prevalence

2. Of the following, documentation will take the form of _____ files during the systems analysis of a computerized data system. 2.____

    A. history
    B. project
    C. case
    D. user

3. Progress notes *usually* contain specific statements concerning each of the following EXCEPT 3.____

    A. response to treatment
    B. medication administration
    C. status at discharge
    D. course of patient's illness

4. Any neonate whose birth occurs from the beginning of the first day (295th day) of the 43rd week following the onset of the last menstrual period is defined as a _____ neonate, according to the World Health Organization's definitions for reporting reproductive health statistics. 4.____

    A. low birthweight
    B. preterm
    C. term
    D. post-term

5. *Box* design forms for handwritten data entry require _____ inch of vertical spacing for each line. 5.____

    A. 1/8
    B. 1/4
    C. 1/3
    D. 1/2

6. Which of the following items would be classified as *interval* data for the purpose of research studies? 6.____

    A. Low/medium/high values
    B. IQ results
    C. True/false responses
    D. 0-100 scale

7. A patient, Jane Q. Brown, born September 5, 1951, is admitted to a health care facility and does not have a Social Security number.
Under the typical *pseudo numbering* system, what would her number be? 7.____

    A. 164-09-0546
    B. 461-46-0905
    C. 367-05-0946
    D. 461-09-0546

8. In 1985, the Joint Commission developed a 10-step process for the quality evaluation of health care facilities.
Which of these steps should be performed LAST by a quality assurance team? 8.____

A. Identify indicators and criteria
B. Delineate scope of care
C. Establish thresholds for evaluation
D. Collect and organize data

9. In conducting peer review of a hospital's activity, a PRO physician would be concerned with each of the following main issues EXCEPT _____ concerns.

   A. DRG B. utilization
   C. ICD-9-CM coding D. quality

10. The purpose of E codes in the Tabular List of the ICD-9-CM classification system is to code for circumstances

    A. particular to obstetric patients and newborns
    B. other than a disease or injury classifiable in the main part of the Tabular List
    C. related to the morphologies and behaviors that are particular to neoplasms
    D. and external environmental events as the cause of injury

11. In designing any form for use in a health information department, the designer of the form should always work PRIMARILY with the _____ in mind.

    A. patient B. provider C. user D. payer

12. In the month of August, 2 of a hospital's 42 patients in the department of medicine died. 5 of 63 surgical patients died in the same month, along with 1 newborn death out of 25 newborns. None of the 25 obstetric patients died in August.
    What was the hospital's patient death rate for August?

    A. 5% B. 8% C. 13% D. 17%

13. According to Medicare requirements, which of the following is a statistical item that should be abstracted from the service data recorded by all hospices?

    A. Average length of bereavement follow-up
    B. Sum total, days of inpatient care received by patients/families
    C. Sum total, days of home care received by patients/families
    D. Average monthly census of each type of service

14. When a hospital's medical staff is NOT organized into units, the data for discharge abstraction should be divided into each of the following categories EXCEPT

    A. medicine B. ancillary C. surgery D. obstetrics

15. Which of the following nomenclature systems was developed PRIMARILY for use with computerized systems?

    A. SNOMED B. CMIT C. SNDO D. CPT-4

16. Of the following, a _____ is NOT typically required to be documented in a mental health patient's emotional or behavioral assessment.

    A. direct psychiatric evaluation
    B. functional evaluation of self-care
    C. vocational and educational history
    D. mental status examination

17. According to the American Health Information Management Association, operative indexes should be retained for a MINIMUM of

   A. 5 years
   B. 10 years
   C. the age of the majority, *plus* the operative statute of limitations
   D. permanently

18. Each of the following is an administrative item that MUST be included in a resident patient's clinical record EXCEPT

   A. property and valuables list
   B. resident's rights acknowledgement
   C. attestation statement
   D. admission agreement

19. Of the following, the _____ is NOT one of the minimum data requirements for a discharge register.

   A. medical record number
   B. admission type
   C. name of the physician
   D. date of discharge or death

20. A hospital discharged 1,251 patients (including deaths; excluding newborns) during April, or a combined length of stay of 6,792 days.
    What was the average length of stay, in days, of the patients discharged during April?

   A. 3   B. 5   C. 6   D. 9

21. Which of the following is a DISADVANTAGE commonly associated with unit numbering and filing systems?

   A. Different elements of a single record may be scattered throughout a single facility or department
   B. Difficulty in retrieving all parts of a single record
   C. Limited provider accessibility
   D. Several folders may be required to house a single record

22. As part of its quality assurance requirements, the Joint Commission expects hospitals to monitor each of the following main categories of activity EXCEPT

   A. medical records
   B. pharmacy
   C. blood usage
   D. aftercare

23. Of the following, _____ information would be included in the systemic inventory of a medical history.

   A. hematologic
   B. present complaint
   C. family history
   D. psychosocial

24. In designing a form where data would be entered with a typewriter, how much horizontal spacing, in inches, should be allowed for each character to accommodate either elite or pica type?

   A. 1/16   B. 2/16   C. 1/12   D. 1/10

25. The *generally* accepted legal principle regarding a medical record is that the content of   25.____
    the record is the property of the

    A. patient
    B. payer
    C. provider
    D. health care institution

KEY (CORRECT ANSWERS)

1. D
2. C
3. B
4. D
5. C

6. B
7. D
8. D
9. C
10. D

11. C
12. A
13. A
14. B
15. A

16. C
17. D
18. C
19. B
20. B

21. D
22. D
23. A
24. D
25. A

TEST 3

DIRECTIONS: Each question or incomplete statement is followed by several suggested answers or completions. Select the one that BEST answers the question or completes the statement. *PRINT THE LETTER OF THE CORRECT ANSWER IN THE SPACE AT THE RIGHT.*

1. In a given time period, the distribution of fifteen of a hospital's inpatient stays was as follows: 5, 1, 2, 3, 4, 5, 3, 1, 2, 1, 5, 1, 18, 8, 1. The total of these stays is 60. What is the MEAN length of stay for this period?

    A. 4   B. 3   C. 2   D. 1

2. Each of the following is an example of occurrence screening EXCEPT

    A. reports of patient dissatisfaction
    B. unplanned injury
    C. neurological deficit at discharge
    D. return to operating room

3. In a health information department, incomplete medical records will have the DISADVANTAGE of being *less* accessible to providers if they are kept in a

    A. permanent file
    B. separate incomplete file, by provider name
    C. separate incomplete file, by medical record number
    D. separate incomplete file, by patient name

4. In a middle digit file, the record number 98-77-55 would be followed by the number

    A. 98-78-55   B. 98-77-56   C. 99-77-55   D. 97-76-54

5. After a patient is discharged, the FIRST element to be removed from the record is typically the

    A. physician's orders   B. medical history
    C. admission form   D. nurse's notes

6. Each of the following is a type of service offered to ambulatory patients by hospitals EXCEPT

    A. ancillary services
    B. rehabilitation services
    C. emergency department
    D. outpatient surgical facilities

7. The discharge summary for a patient in a mental health institution should be made within _____ of the patient's discharge.

    A. 48 hours   B. 72 hours   C. 15 days   D. 30 days

8. Which of the following types of graphic data presentations ALWAYS represents a percentage?

A. Bar graph B. Histogram
C. Pie graph D. Line graph

9. Which of the following forms would be considered *optional* (depending upon the operation) for inclusion in a patient's medical record prior to surgery?

   A. Imaging report B. Medical history
   C. Preoperative diagnosis D. Physical exam

10. Of the following data control procedures, _____ measures the performance of data, compares it with existing standards, and acts on any differences.

    A. specifying standards B. abstract review
    C. quality control D. audit

11. When using the COSTAR system, problems classified as *minor* are entered into the system with the symbol

    A. M B. m C. V' D. 0

12. In a typical color-coded filing system, an orange band would signify the two-digit primary numbers from

    A. 00-09 B. 30-39 C. 50-59 D. 90-99

13. Of the following, _____ of all errors is NOT a universal purpose of controls that is considered to ensure data accuracy in a computerized system.

    A. detecting the existence
    B. location
    C. providing for correction
    D. making necessary correction

14. In designing a form, the form identification and edition date appear

    A. at the top right
    B. in the lower right margin
    C. at the top left
    D. in the lower left margin

15. Approximately _____ weeks should be allowed, after the placement of an order, for a quantity of single-part forms (smaller than 11" x 17") to be implemented.

    A. 2-3 B. 3-4 C. 4-8 D. 8-12

16. Which of the following classification systems is MOST commonly used to code the diagnoses and treatments of mental health patients?

    A. DSM-IV B. AAMD C. HCPCS D. ICD-M

17. In most computerized chart location systems, each of the following is a required entry for signing out a record EXCEPT

    A. patient name B. record number
    C. department code D. reason code

18. The progress notes of a problem-oriented medical record may contain each of the following types of information EXCEPT

A. symptomatic information B. objective information
C. transfer notes D. demographic problems

19. Master Patient Indexes using a phonetic filing system appear MOSTLY in facilities

    A. serving a community where there is a large number of foreign names
    B. utilizing scant personnel resources
    C. that already have a unit numbering system in place
    D. serving a patient population of over 100,000 patients

20. Which of the following issues relating to AIDS-related diseases is of LEAST concern to health information practitioners?

    A. Proper coding B. Disease etiology
    C. Disclosure D. Reporting requirements

21. Several copies of a form that are prefastened and collated are known as a _____ set.

    A. form B. unit C. stub D. fanfold

22. In a middle digit filing system application of family number 03-789624, the PRIMARY digits are

    A. 03 B. 78 C. 96 D. 89

23. Which of the following is NOT one of the four basic methods used by health information departments for the release of authorized information from medical records?

    A. Direct access
    B. Abstracting information
    C. Distribution of algorithmic coding passwords
    D. Verbal release

24. A *qualitative* analysis of medical record documentation is used PRIMARILY in order to

    A. identify areas of the record that are incomplete
    B. abstract data to aid clinical or administrative decision-making
    C. identify obvious and routine omissions in the record
    D. identify inconsistent or inaccurate documentation

25. In resident nursing facilities, the drug regimen of each patient MUST be reviewed _____ by a licensed pharmacist.

    A. monthly B. quarterly
    C. biannually D. annually

KEY (CORRECT ANSWERS)

1. A
2. A
3. A
4. B
5. D

6. B
7. C
8. C
9. A
10. C

11. B
12. B
13. D
14. D
15. B

16. A
17. C
18. D
19. A
20. B

21. A
22. C
23. C
24. D
25. A

EXAMINATION SECTION
TEST 1

DIRECTIONS: Each question or incomplete statement is followed by several suggested answers or completions. Select the one that BEST answers the question or completes the statement. *PRINT THE LETTER OF THE CORRECT ANSWER IN THE SPACE AT THE RIGHT.*

1. In filing records by subject, you should be MOST concerned with the

   A. name of the sender
   B. main topic of the letter
   C. date of the correspondence
   D. alphabetic cross reference

2. When arranging the medical record cards of patients in alphabetical order, the one of the following which should be filed THIRD is

   A. Charles A. Clarke   B. James Clark
   C. Joan Carney   D. Mae Cohen

3. The one of the following names which should be filed FIRST is

   A. Benjamin Dermody   B. Frank Davidson
   C. Matthew Davids   D. Seymour Diana

4. Vital statistics include data relating to

   A. births, deaths, and marriages
   B. the cost of food, clothing, and shelter
   C. the number of children per family unit
   D. diseases and their comparative mortality rates

Questions 5-10.

DIRECTIONS: Questions 5 through 10 are to be answered on the basis of the usual rules for alphabetical filing. For each question, indicate in the space at the right the letter preceding the name which should be filed THIRD in alphabetical order.

5. A. Hesselberg, Norman J.   B. Hesselman, Nathan B.
   C. Hazel, Robert S.   D. Heintz, August J.

6. A. Oshins, Jerome   B. O'Shaugn, F.J.
   C. O'Shaugn, F.J.   D. O'Shea, Frances

7. A. Petrie, Joshua A.   B. Pendleton, Oscar
   C. Pertwee, Joshua   D. Perkins, Warren G.

8. A. Morganstern, Alfred   B. Morganstern, Albert
   C. Monroe, Mildred   D. Modesti, Ernest

9. A. More, Stewart   B. Moorhead, Jay
   C. Moore, Benjamin   D. Moffat, Edith

10. A. Ramirez, Paul B. Revere, Pauline   10.____
    C. Ramos, Felix   D. Ramazotti, Angelo

Questions 11-20.

DIRECTIONS: Questions 11 through 20 are to be answered on the basis of the usual rules of filing. Column I lists, next to the numbers 11 to 20, the names of 10 clinic patients. Column II lists, next to the letters A to D, the headings of file drawers into which you are to place the medical records of these patients. For each question, indicate in the space at the right the letter preceding the heading of the file drawer in which the record should be filed.

COLUMN I   COLUMN II

11. Charles Coughlin   A. Cab-Cep   11.____
12. Mary Carstairs   B. Ceq-Cho   12.____
13. Joseph Collin   C. Chr-Coj   13.____
14. Thomas Chelsey   D. Cok-Czy   14.____
15. Cedric Chalmers   15.____
16. Mae Clarke   16.____
17. Dora Copperhead   17.____
18. Arnold Cohn   18.____
19. Charlotte Crumboldt   19.____
20. Frances Celine   20.____

Questions 21-25.

DIRECTIONS: Questions 21 through 25 are to be answered on the basis of the chart below.

ATTENDANCE OF PATIENTS AT Y HEALTH CENTER
FOR WEEK OF APRIL 10

CLINIC	NUMBER SUMMONED FOR				NUMBER REPORTED TO			
	BABY	CHEST	EYE	V.D.	BABY	CHEST	EYE	V.D.
Monday	30	42	36	38	29	40	33	35
Tuesday	33	29	34	37	30	29	31	36
Wednesday	38	31	45	42	35	30	40	40
Thursday	41	48	41	32	36	45	39	28
Friday	35	37	39	36	33	35	37	32

21. On the basis of the above chart, it is CORRECT to say that _____ Clinic during the week.   21._____

    A. more patients were summoned to the Baby Clinic than to the Chest
    B. the same number of patients were absent from the Eye Clinic and the Baby
    C. more patients reported to the Eye Clinic than to the Chest
    D. more patients were summoned to the V.D. Clinic than to the Eye

22. On the basis of the above chart, the daily average number of patients summoned to the Eye Clinic exceeds the daily average reporting to the Eye Clinic by   22._____

    A. 3   B. 7   C. 11   D. 15

23. The percentage of all patients summoned to Y Health Center on Thursday who failed to report for their appointments is   23._____

    A. less than 5%
    B. more than 5% but less than 10%
    C. more than 10% but less than 15%
    D. more than 15%

24. The number of patients summoned for the entire week to the Eye Clinic exceeds the number of patients summoned to the Baby Clinic by   24._____

    A. 6   B. 9   C. 13   D. 18

25. The total number of patients who reported to Y Health Center for the week is   25._____

    A. 683   B. 693   C. 724   D. 744

KEY (CORRECT ANSWERS)

1. B   11. D
2. A   12. A
3. C   13. D
4. A   14. B
5. A   15. B

6. D   16. C
7. C   17. D
8. B   18. C
9. B   19. D
10. C   20. A

21. C
22. A
23. B
24. D
25. B

TEST 2

DIRECTIONS: Each question or incomplete statement is followed by several suggested answers or completions. Select the one that BEST answers the question or completes the statement. *PRINT THE LETTER OF THE CORRECT ANSWER IN THE SPACE AT THE RIGHT.*

Questions 1-8.

DIRECTIONS: Questions 1 through 8 are to be answered on the basis of the usual rules of filing. Column I lists, next to the numbers 1 to 8, the names of 8 clinic patients. Column II lists, next to the letters A to O, the headings of file drawers into which you are to place the records of these patients. In the space at the right, corresponding to each name listed in Column I, print the letter preceding the heading of the file drawer in which the record should be filed.

COLUMN I		COLUMN II	
1. Thomas Adams	A.	Aab-Abi	1.____
2. Joseph Albert	B.	Abj-Ach	2.____
3. Frank Anaster	C.	Aci-Aco	3.____
4. Charles Abt	D.	Acp-Ada	4.____
5. John Alfred	E.	Adb-Afr	5.____
6. Louis Aron	F.	Afs-Ago	6.____
7. Francis Amos	G.	Agp-Ahz	7.____
8. William Adler	H.	Aia-Ako	8.____
	I.	Akp-Ald	
	J.	Ale-Amo	
	K.	Amp-Aor	
	L.	Aos-Apr	
	M.	Aps-Asi	
	N.	Asj-Ati	
	O.	Atj-Awz	

Questions 9-14.

DIRECTIONS: In answering Questions 9 through 14, alphabetize the four names listed in each question; then print in the corresponding space at the right the letter of the answer containing the four numbers preceding the alphabetized names to show the CORRECT alphabetical arrangement of the four names.

9. 1. Frank Adam   2. Frank Aarons   9._____
    3. Frank Aaron   4. Frank Adams
    The CORRECT answer is:

    A. 2, 3, 1, 4   B. 4, 2, 1, 3
    C. 1, 2, 4, 3   D. 3, 2, 1, 4

10. 1. Richard Lavine   2. Richard Levine   10._____
    3. Edward Lawrence   4. Edward Loraine
    The CORRECT answer is:

    A. 1, 2, 3, 4   B. 3, 1, 2, 4
    C. 1, 3, 2, 4   D. 2, 4, 3, 1

11. 1. G. Frank Adam   2. Frank Adam   11._____
    3. Fanny Adam   4. Franklin Adam
    The CORRECT answer is:

    A. 3, 4, 1, 2   B. 2, 1, 3, 4
    C. 3, 2, 4, 1   D. 2, 3, 4, 1

12. 1. George Cohn   2. Richard Cohen   12._____
    3. Thomas Cohane   4. George Cohan
    The CORRECT answer is:

    A. 2, 1, 3, 4   B. 4, 1, 3, 2
    C. 3, 1, 4, 2   D. 4, 3, 2, 1

13. 1. Paul Shultz   2. Robert Schmid   13._____
    3. Joseph Schwartz   4. Edward Schmidt
    The CORRECT answer is:

    A. 2, 4, 3, 1   B. 2, 1, 3, 4
    C. 3, 4, 1, 2   D. 1, 2, 4, 3

14. 1. Peter Consilazio   2. Frank Consolezio   14._____
    3. Robert Consalizio 4. Ella Consolizio
    The CORRECT answer is:

    A. 3, 4, 1, 2   B. 3, 1, 2, 4
    C. 1, 2, 4, 3   D. 3, 2, 1, 4

Questions 15-25.

DIRECTIONS: For Questions 15 through 25, select the letter preceding the word which means MOST NEARLY the same as the word in capitals.

15. LEGIBLE   15._____

    A. readable   B. eligible   C. learned   D. lawful

16. OBSERVE   16._____

    A. assist   B. watch   C. correct   D. oppose

17. HABITUAL   17._____

    A. punctual   B. occasional
    C. usual   D. actual

18. CHRONOLOGICAL

    A. successive   B. earlier
    C. later   D. studious

19. ARREST

    A. punish   B. run   C. threaten   D. stop

20. ABSTAIN

    A. refrain   B. indulge   C. discolor   D. spoil

21. TOXIC

    A. poisonous   B. decaying
    C. taxing   D. defective

22. TOLERATE

    A. fear   B. forgive   C. allow   D. despise

23. VENTILATE

    A. vacate   B. air   C. extricate   D. heat

24. SUPERIOR

    A. perfect   B. subordinate
    C. lower   D. higher

25. EXTREMITY

    A. extent   B. limb   C. illness   D. execution

KEY (CORRECT ANSWERS)

1. D
2. I
3. K
4. B
5. J

6. M
7. J
8. E
9. D
10. C

11. C
12. D
13. A
14. B
15. A

16. B
17. C
18. A
19. D
20. A

21. A
22. C
23. B
24. D
25. B

TEST 3

DIRECTIONS: Each question or incomplete statement is followed by several suggested answers or completions. Select the one that BEST answers the question or completes the statement. *PRINT THE LETTER OF THE CORRECT ANSWER IN THE SPACE AT THE RIGHT.*

Questions 1-20.

DIRECTIONS: Column I below lists words used in medical practice. Column II lists phrases which describe the words in Column I. In the space at the right, opposite the number preceding each of the words in Column I, place the letter preceding the phrase in Column II which BEST describes the word in Column I.

COLUMN I

1. Abrasion
2. Aseptic
3. Cardiac
4. Catarrh
5. Contamination
6. Dermatology
7. Disinfectant
8. Dyspepsia
9. Epidemic
10. Epidermis
11. Incubation
12. Microscope
13. Pediatrics
14. Plasma
15. Prenatal
16. Retina
17. Syphilis
18. Syringe
19. Toxemia
20. Vaccine

COLUMN II

A. A disturbance of digestion
B. Destroying the germs of disease
C. A general poisoning of the blood
D. An instrument used for injecting fluids
E. A scraping off of the skin
F. Free from disease germs
G. An apparatus for viewing internal organs by means of x-rays
H. An instrument for assisting the eye in observing minute objects
I. An inoculable immunizing agent
J. The extensive prevalence in a community of a disease
K. Chemical product of an organ
L. Preceding birth
M. Fever
N. Branch of medical science that relates to skin and its diseases
O. Fluid part of the blood
P. The science of hygienic care of children
Q. Infection by contact
R. Relating to the heart
S. Inner structure of the eye
T. Outer portion of the skin
U. Pertaining to the ductless glands
V. An infectious venereal disease
X. The development of an infectious disease from the period of infection to that of the appearance of the first symptoms
Y. Simple inflammation of a mucous membrane
Z. An instrument for measuring blood pressure

1. ____
2. ____
3. ____
4. ____
5. ____
6. ____
7. ____
8. ____
9. ____
10. ____
11. ____
12. ____
13. ____
14. ____
15. ____
16. ____
17. ____
18. ____
19. ____
20. ____

21. The fluoroscope is used CHIEFLY to 21.____
   A. provide a permanent picture of the condition of internal organs at a given time
   B. make a chart of the action of the muscles of the heart
   C. observe the internal structure and functioning of the organs of the body at a given time
   D. produce heat in the tissues of the body

22. A stethoscope is an instrument used for 22.____
   A. determining the blood pressure
   B. taking the body temperature
   C. chest examinations
   D. determining the amount of sugar in the blood

23. The Dick test is used to determine susceptibility to 23.____
   A. measles   B. scarlet fever
   C. diphtheria   D. chicken pox

24. The aorta is a(n) 24.____
   A. bone   B. artery   C. ligament   D. nerve

25. The esophagus is part of the 25.____
   A. alimentary canal   B. abdominal wall
   C. mucous membrane   D. circulatory system

KEY (CORRECT ANSWERS)

1. E
2. F
3. R
4. Y
5. Q

6. N
7. B
8. A
9. J
10. T

11. X
12. H
13. P
14. O
15. L

16. S
17. V
18. D
19. C
20. I

21. C
22. C
23. B
24. B
25. A

EXAMINATION SECTION
TEST 1

DIRECTIONS: Each question or incomplete statement is followed by several suggested answers or completions. Select the one that BEST answers the question or completes the statement. *PRINT THE LETTER OF THE CORRECT ANSWER IN THE SPACE AT THE RIGHT.*

1. Assume that you are working in an admitting office near the main entrance of a hospital. Visitors often come into your office to ask questions about hospital procedures and your supervisor has told you to be as helpful as possible in these situations.
   If a visitor comes in and asks you some questions about hospital procedures in a loud and emotional voice, the BEST course of action for you to take would be to

   A. ask him to leave the hospital and come back when he can control himself
   B. ask him to write the questions on a sheet of paper
   C. remain calm and try to answer his questions
   D. tell him to calm down or you will not answer any questions

   1.____

2. A certain hospital office administers a community health program in which members of the public are enrolled. There has been a recent change of procedure in the program and the office expects to receive a large number of letters from those enrolled asking about the change.
   Of the following, the MOST appropriate method of answering these letters is to

   A. invite each person who sends in a letter to come to the office so that the change can be explained in a personal interview
   B. prepare a form letter which explains the change of procedure and send a copy to each person who sends in a letter
   C. stamp the notation *Procedure Changed/Please Comply* on each letter and mail it back to the sender together with a description of the change of procedure
   D. telephone each person who sends in a letter and explain the change of procedure

   2.____

3. Assume that you work in a business office of a hospital and your supervisor gives you an assignment to be completed in one week. Part of the assignment requires you to obtain information from the various departments of the hospital. All departments have cooperated in giving you the required information, except one. Despite your repeated attempts to secure the information, it is still missing the day before your assignment is scheduled for completion. Even if you received the missing information immediately, you could not complete the assignment on time.
   Of the following, the FIRST action you should take in this situation is to

   A. advise your supervisor that you were not given enough time to complete the assignment
   B. contact the department which has the information you need and tell them that their failure to cooperate has made it impossible for you to complete your assignment on time
   C. explain to your supervisor why you cannot complete the assignment on time and ask him if he wishes to receive what you will be able to finish
   D. tell your supervisor that you will try to finish the assignment whenever the information is forthcoming

   3.____

4. Suppose that you work in a hospital office and you are speaking on the telephone with another employee on hospital business. While you are speaking on the telephone, a co-worker enters the office and indicates that she would like to speak with you.
Of the following, the BEST course of action for you to take in this situation is to

   A. excuse yourself on the telephone and ask your co-worker to wait until you are finished with the call
   B. ignore your co-worker and continue your telephone conversation
   C. immediately end your telephone conversation and tell your co-worker not to interrupt you again when you are speaking on the telephone
   D. tell the employee on the telephone that you have to speak with someone else and will call back as soon as you are finished

5. Assume that you are in charge of the petty cash fund for your office. When an individual wants to be paid back for an expense, he must complete a receipt explaining the expense and sign the receipt when you give him the money. One day, a clerk in your office tells you that she has just returned after delivering a package and wants to be paid back immediately for the carfare she spent. The clerk says that she has a lot of work to do in the next few hours and will complete the receipt later in the day. The BEST course of action for you to take in this situation is to

   A. explain to her that in order to receive the money she must complete and sign the receipt
   B. give her the money and leave a note on her desk reminding her to complete and sign the receipt
   C. give her the money and leave a note for yourself to make sure that she completes and signs the receipt
   D. tell her that you will give her the money and that you will complete the receipt yourself

6. Suppose that you have recently been assigned to an office and that one of your tasks is to keep files in proper order. You observe that some of your co-workers remove folders from the files, with no indication of removal. These actions have made it difficult for you to locate the folders when you need them.
Of the following, the MOST desirable method of correcting this situation is to

   A. make photocopies of the materials in all the folders and organize a duplicate set of files so that you will always have the folders readily available
   B. make sure that there are enough out-guides available and that everyone in the office is instructed to use them whenever a folder is removed
   C. tell your co-workers that they can use the files only after they tell you what folders they are going to remove
   D. ask your co-workers to leave a note on your desk whenever anyone removes a folder from the files

7. Of the following, the LEAST desirable action to take when writing out a check to a person is to

   A. fill out the check in pencil
   B. date the check
   C. number the check
   D. write the person's full name

Questions 8-17.

DIRECTIONS: Questions 8 through 17 each show in Column I names written on four cards (lettered w, x, y, z) which have to be filed. You are to choose the option (lettered A, B, C, or D) in Column II which BEST represents the proper order of filing according to the rules and sample question given below. The cards are to filed according to the following Rules for Alphabetical Filing.

RULES FOR ALPHABETICAL FILING

1. The names of individuals are filed in strict alphabetical order, first according to the last name, then according to first name or initial, and finally according to middle name or initial. For example: George Allen precedes Edward Bell; Leonard Reston precedes Lucille Reston.

2. When last names are the same, for example, A. Green and Agnes Green, the one with the initial comes before the one with the name written out when the first initials are identical.

3. When first and last names are the same, a name without a middle initial comes before one with a middle initial. For example: Ralph Simon comes before both Ralph A. Simon and Ralph Adam Simon.

4. When first and last names are the same, a name with a middle initial comes before one with a middle name beginning with the same initial. For example: Sam P. Rogers comes before Sam Paul Rogers.

5. Prefixes such as De, O', Mac, Mc, and Van are filed as written and are treated as part of the names to which they are connected. For example: Gladys McTeaque is filed before Frances Meadows.

6. Titles and designations such as Dr., Mr., and Prof, are ignored in filing.

SAMPLE QUESTION

COLUMN I

w. Jane Earl
x. James A. Earle
y. James Earl
z. J. Earle

COLUMN II

A. w, y, z, x
B. y, w, z, x
C. x, y, w, z
D. x, w, y, z

The correct way to file the cards is:
y. James Earl
w. Jane Earl
z. J. Earle
x. James A. Earle

The correct filing order is shown by the letters y, w, z, x (in that order). Since, in Column II, B appears in front of the letters y, w, z, x (in that order), B is the correct answer to the sample question.

Now answer Questions 8 through 17 using the same procedure.

COLUMN I			COLUMN II		
8.	w.	John Smith	A.	w, x, y, z	8.____
	x.	Joan Smythe	B.	y, z, x, w	
	y.	Gerald Schmidt	C.	y, z, w, x	
	z.	Gary Schmitt	D.	z, y, w, x	
9.	w.	A. Black	A.	w, x, y, z	9.____
	x.	Alan S. Black	B.	w, y, x, z	
	y.	Allan Black	C.	w, y, z, x	
	z.	Allen A. Black	D.	x, w, y, z	
10.	w.	Samuel Haynes	A.	w, x, y, z	10.____
	x.	Sam C. Haynes	B.	x, w, z, y	
	y.	David Haynes	C.	y, z, w, x	
	z.	Dave L. Haynes	D.	z, y, x, w	
11.	w.	Lisa B. McNeil	A.	x, y, w, z	11.____
	x.	Tom MacNeal	B.	x, z, y, w	
	y.	Lisa McNeil	C.	y, w, z, x	
	z.	Lorainne McNeal	D.	z, x, y, w	
12.	w.	Larry Richardson	A.	w, y, x, z	12.____
	x.	Leroy Richards	B.	y, x, z, w	
	y.	Larry S. Richards	C.	y, z, x, w	
	z.	Leroy C. Richards	D.	x, w, z, y	
13.	w.	Arlene Lane	A.	w, z, y, x	13.____
	x.	Arlene Cora Lane	B.	w, z, x, y	
	y.	Arlene Clair Lane	C.	y, x, z, w	
	z.	Arlene C. Lane	D.	z, y, w, x	
14.	w.	Betty Fish	A.	w, x, z, y	14.____
	x.	Prof. Ann Fish	B.	x, w, y, z	
	y.	Norma Fisch	C.	y, z, x, w	
	z.	Dr. Richard Fisch	D.	z, y, w, x	
15.	w.	Dr. Anthony David Lukak	A.	w, y, z, x	15.____
	x.	Mr. Steven Charles Lucas	B.	x, z, w, y	
	y.	Mr. Anthony J. Lukak	C.	z, x, y, w	
	z.	Prof. Steven C. Lucas	D.	z, x, w, y	
16.	w.	Martha Y. Lind	A.	w, y, z, x	16.____
	x.	Mary Beth Linden	B.	w, y, x, z	
	y.	Martha W. Lind	C.	y, w, z, x	
	z.	Mary Bertha Linden	D.	y, w, x, z	
17.	w.	Prof. Harry Michael MacPhelps	A.	w, z, x, y	17.____
	x.	Mr. Horace M. MacPherson	B.	w, y, z, x	
	y.	Mr. Harold M. McPhelps	C.	z, x, w, y	
	z.	Prof. Henry Martin MacPherson	D.	x, z, y, w	

18. Assume that one of your duties is to make sure that the office supply cabinet contains sufficient quantities of the forms used in your office.
Of the following, the BEST course of action for you to adopt in order to be able to perform this duty is to

    A. ask your supervisor each day whether the office is low on any form and plan to order only those forms which are mentioned
    B. decide what kind of duplicating equipment will be needed to produce copies of the forms when the current supply is exhausted
    C. plan for your office's needs and order copies of the forms before the number of copies in the cabinet falls below a minimum amount
    D. wait until one of your co-workers tells you that the office is running short of a form and then obtain copies of it as quickly as possible

19. The type of file in which reports are found under the heading *New York State-Queens* is MOST likely to be a _____ file.

    A. chronological   B. geographic
    C. numeric   D. tickler

20. Assume that you are working in the personnel office of a hospital. One day, you answer a telephone call and the caller asks to speak to one of your co-workers, Ms. Wilson, who is on sick leave. You explain this to the caller who then tells you that she is a friend of Ms. Wilson's and would like to invite her to a party but has lost Ms. Wilson's home address and telephone number. The caller then asks you if you can give her this information.
Of the following, the BEST course of action for you to take then is to

    A. give the caller the information and then leave Ms. Wilson a message about the telephone call
    B. decline to give the caller the information and ask the caller if she wants to leave a message for Ms. Wilson
    C. tell the caller that all information about hospital employees is confidential and that you cannot spend any more time on a personal telephone call
    D. tell the caller that you need some time to look up the information and ask her to call back later in the day

KEY (CORRECT ANSWERS)

1. C
2. B
3. C
4. A
5. A

6. B
7. A
8. C
9. A
10. D

11. B
12. B
13. A
14. C
15. D

16. C
17. A
18. C
19. B
20. B

TEST 2

DIRECTIONS: Each question or incomplete statement is followed by several suggested answers or completions. Select the one that BEST answers the question or completes the statement. *PRINT THE LETTER OF THE CORRECT ANSWER IN THE SPACE AT THE RIGHT.*

1. Suppose that you answer a telephone call and a woman asks to speak with your supervisor. Your supervisor, however, is speaking with someone on another telephone line.
   Of the following, the BEST course of action for you to take in this situation is to

   A. ask the caller for her name and telephone number and tell her that your supervisor will return the call as soon as possible
   B. ask the caller to call again later in the day because your supervisor is busy right now
   C. explain to the caller why your supervisor cannot answer the call and ask her to wait until your supervisor can speak with her
   D. tell the caller that your supervisor is speaking on another line and ask her if she wants to wait until that call is finished or wants to leave a message

2. One morning, you receive a telephone call and the caller requests an appointment with your supervisor. Your supervisor is out of the office for the day. You tell the caller that she can meet with your supervisor at 10 A.M. the next day and she agrees. After ending this telephone conversation, you discover that your supervisor already has scheduled an appointment with someone else for that time.
   Of the following, the BEST course of action for you to take in this situation is to

   A. contact your supervisor and find out which appointment he would rather keep
   B. decide which appointment is less important and cancel it
   C. try to change the appointment you made for the caller to another time
   D. wait until the next day and then tell your supervisor that he has a choice of two appointments scheduled at 10 A.M.

3. Assume that your supervisor has asked you to go to the stockroom to pick up supplies that your office has ordered. Of the following, the FIRST action you should take when you are given the supplies is to

   A. bring the supplies back to your office immediately
   B. call your supervisor to find out whether any other supplies are needed
   C. check to see whether you have received everything that was ordered
   D. sign a receipt for the supplies

Questions 4-8.

DIRECTIONS: In each of Questions 4 through 8, there is a sentence containing one underlined word. Choose the word (lettered A, B, C, or D) which means MOST NEARLY the same as the underlined word as it is used in the sentence.

4. The number of applicants exceeded the <u>anticipated</u> figure.

   A. expected   B. required   C. revised   D. necessary

5. The clerk was told to <u>collate</u> the pages of the report.

   A. destroy   B. edit   C. correct   D. assemble

6. Mr. Wells is not <u>authorized</u> to release the information.

   A. inclined   B. pleased   C. permitted   D. trained

7. The secretary chose an <u>appropriate</u> office for the meeting.

   A. empty   B. decorated   C. nearby   D. suitable

8. The employee performs a <u>complex</u> set of tasks each day.

   A. difficult   B. important   C. pleasant   D. large

9. Of the following, the MOST important purpose of a filing system generally is to

   A. reduce the number of records which must be readily available
   B. make it possible to locate information quickly
   C. organize material under the fewest number of headings
   D. provide a secure storage place if an unexpected emergency occurs

10. Assume that you answer a telephone call and the caller wishes to speak to one of your co-workers, who is out of the office.
    Of the following, the LEAST appropriate information for you to indicate on a message which you leave for your co-worker is

    A. the caller's telephone number and extension
    B. the date and time the call was received
    C. the office telephone on which the call was received
    D. your name or initials

11. The notation *cc: Mr. Rogers* appearing at the bottom of a letter is MOST likely to indicate that Mr. Rogers

    A. typed the letter
    B. is the subject of the letter
    C. wrote the rough draft of the letter for his supervisor
    D. is to receive a copy of the letter

Questions 12-16.

DIRECTIONS: Questions 12 through 16 are to be answered ONLY on the basis of the information provided in the following passage.

For some office workers, it is useful to be familiar with the four main classes of domestic mail; for others, it is essential. Each class has a different rate of postage and some have requirements concerning wrapping, sealing or special information to be placed on the package. First class mail, the class which may not be opened for postal inspection, includes letters, postcards, business reply cards, and other kinds of written matter. There are different rates for some of the kinds of cards which can be sent by first class mail. The maximum weight for an item sent by first class mail is 70 pounds. An item which is not letter size should be marked *First Class* on all sides.

Although office workers most often come into contact with first class mail, they may find it helpful to know something about the other classes. Second class mail is generally used for mailing newspapers and magazines. Publishers of these articles must meet certain U.S. Postal Service requirements in order to obtain a permit to use second class mailing rates. Third class mail, which must weigh less than 1 pound, includes printed materials and merchandise parcels. There are two rate structures for this class, a single piece rate and a bulk rate. Fourth class mail, also known as parcel post, includes packages weighing from one to 40 pounds. For more information about these classes of mail and the actual mailing rates, contact your local post office.

12. According to this passage, first class mail is the only class which

    A. has a limit on the maximum weight of an item
    B. has different rates for items within the class
    C. may not be opened for postal inspection
    D. should be used by office workers

13. According to this passage, the one of the following items which may correctly be sent by fourth class mail is a

    A. magazine weighing one-half pound
    B. package weighing one-half pound
    C. package weighing two pounds
    D. postcard

14. According to this passage, there are different postage rates for

    A. a newspaper sent by second class mail and a magazine sent by second class mail
    B. each of the classes of mail
    C. each pound of fourth class mail
    D. printed material sent by third class mail and merchandise parcels sent by third class mail

15. In order to send a newspaper by second class mail, a publisher must

    A. have met certain postal requirements and obtained a permit
    B. indicate whether he wants to use the single piece or the bulk rate
    C. make certain that the newspaper weighs less than one pound
    D. mark the newspaper *Second Class* on the top and bottom of the wrapper

16. Of the following types of information, the one which is NOT mentioned in the passage is the

    A. class of mail to which parcel post belongs
    B. kinds of items which can be sent by each class of mail
    C. maximum weight for an item sent by fourth class mail
    D. postage rate for each of the four classes of mail

17. Assume that one of your tasks is to complete a form indicating which laboratory test a doctor is ordering.
    A doctor has written an order for a laboratory test, but his writing is illegible, and you cannot tell which of two tests he is ordering.
    Of the following, the BEST course of action for you to take in this situation is to

A. show the doctor his written order, ask the doctor which test he meant to order, and then fill out the form
B. indicate both tests on the form so that you will be certain that the correct test is performed
C. send the doctor's written order to the laboratory without indicating on the form which test is to be done, since the laboratory technician will know from experience which test the doctor meant to order
D. wait for the doctor to reorder the test when he finds out that it has not been done

18. Suppose that one of your tasks is to mail an application form and covering letter to each applicant for a program administered by your office.
Of the following, the MOST appropriate notation to use at the bottom of the letter to indicate that the form is included in the envelope is

   A. Enc.　　　B. etc.　　　C. P.S.　　　D. R.S.V.P.

19. Of the following, the LEAST appropriate practice involved in the proper use of a file cabinet and its contents is to

   A. close a cabinet drawer immediately after using it
   B. place active files in top drawers and less active files in bottom drawers
   C. remove a file folder by holding the side of the folder, not the tab
   D. store office supplies behind files in unfilled cabinet drawers

20. Assume that you are sending out a business letter and have to write *Attention: Mrs. Williams* on the envelope. Of the following, the PROPER place on the envelope for you to write this notation is the _____ of the envelope.

   A. upper right corner of the back
   B. upper right corner on the front
   C. lower left corner of the back
   D. lower left corner on the front

KEY (CORRECT ANSWERS)

1.	D	11.	D
2.	C	12.	C
3.	C	13.	C
4.	A	14.	B
5.	D	15.	A
6.	C	16.	D
7.	D	17.	A
8.	A	18.	A
9.	B	19.	D
10.	C	20.	D

TEST 3

DIRECTIONS: Each question or incomplete statement is followed by several suggested answers or completions. Select the one that BEST answers the question or completes the statement. *PRINT THE LETTER OF THE CORRECT ANSWER IN THE SPACE AT THE RIGHT.*

1. Which of the following is the MOST efficient method of reproducing 50 copies of a single-page form letter?

    A. Carbon copying
    B. Scanning and re-editing
    C. Word processing
    D. Photocopying

2. Removing inactive documents from the active files and transferring them to a records storage center is important for which of the following reasons?

    A. The active records can be filed and retrieved more quickly.
    B. The inactive files will no longer be needed.
    C. No control is necessary with respect to the inactive files.
    D. It allows you to know which documents must be filed and which need not be filed.

3. You are trying to obtain information from someone who is to be admitted to a hospital. The person tells you in an angry tone of voice that he will not give you a certain item of information. You need this information to complete the admission form.
   Of the following, the FIRST action which you should take in this situation is to

    A. tell him that he will not be admitted unless he gives you the information
    B. tell him to wait while you go asks your supervisor to get the information from the person
    C. leave out that item of information but clearly show your anger so he will not act that way again
    D. tell him the reason why you need that item of information

4. Assume that you work in a hospital office which often receives telephone calls from people requesting information about patients in the hospital. One day, you receive a telephone call from a person who says that he is the brother of a patient. The caller asks you what is wrong with the patient and how long he will remain in the hospital.
   Of the following, the BEST course of action for you to take in this situation is to

    A. check the patient's hospital records to make sure the patient has a brother and then give the caller the information he requested
    B. contact the patient's doctor to get the information and then give it to the caller
    C. inform the caller that you are not permitted to give out that information and refer him to the patient's doctor
    D. tell the caller that you will have to check the hospital records to get the information and ask the caller for his telephone number so that you can call him back

Questions 5-14.

DIRECTIONS: Questions 5 through 14 are based on the following table, which shows the number of persons admitted to and discharged from each of five hospitals for each of the first six months of 2005. Admissions are shown under the columns labeled *ADM* and discharges under the columns labeled *DIS*.

ADMISSIONS AND DISCHARGES
January-June, 2005

MONTH	HOSPITAL L ADM	HOSPITAL L DIS	HOSPITAL M ADM	HOSPITAL M DIS	HOSPITAL N ADM	HOSPITAL N DIS	HOSPITAL O ADM	HOSPITAL O DIS	HOSPITAL P ADM	HOSPITAL P DIS
JAN.	367	291	389	372	738	694	1101	942	1567	1373
FEB.	447	473	411	376	874	841	1353	1296	1754	1687
MAR.	426	437	403	436	831	813	1297	1358	1690	1740
APR.	403	390	370	385	794	850	1057	1190	1389	1650
MAY	370	411	361	390	680	692	984	1039	1195	1210
JUNE	334	355	377	384	630	619	1121	1043	1125	1065

5. The TOTAL number of admissions to the five hospitals for the month of April was

    A. 3,833   B. 3,952   C. 3,983   D. 4,013

5.___

6. The TOTAL number of discharges from Hospital N for the months of April, May, and June was

    A. 1,159   B. 2,104   C. 2,161   D. 2,251

6.___

7. The TOTAL number of admissions to Hospitals L, M, and O for the month of February was

    A. 1,732   B. 2,101   C. 2,145   D. 2,211

7.___

8. The TOTAL number of discharges from the five hospitals for the month of January was

    A. 3,542   B. 3,672   C. 3,832   D. 4,162

8.___

9. For which month were there MORE discharges at each of the five hospitals than there were admissions?

    A. January   B. March   C. May   D. June

9.___

10. The average number of admissions each month at Hospital O for the first six months of 2005 was MOST NEARLY

    A. 1,097   B. 1,152   C. 1,163   D. 1,196

10.___

11. Of the total number of admissions at the five hospitals for the month of March, what percentage, to the nearest whole percent, was admitted to Hospital P?

    A. 29%   B. 32%   C. 34%   D. 36%

11.___

12. The average number of discharges from each of the five hospitals for the month of May was MOST NEARLY

    A. 748   B. 754   C. 762   D. 764

12.___

13. Of the total number of admissions to the five hospitals for the month of June, what percentage, to the nearest whole percent, was admitted to Hospital M?

    A. 7%   B. 9%   C. 11%   D. 13%

13.___

14. On the basis of the information given in the table, which one of the following statements is CORRECT?
    The number of

    A. admissions to each hospital for the month of April was less than the number of admissions for the month of March
    B. admissions to Hospital L increased each month from January through April and decreased each month from May through June
    C. discharges from each hospital for the month of June was less than the number of discharges for the month of May
    D. discharges from Hospital O increased each month from January through March and decreased each month from April through June

14._____

Questions 15-20.

DIRECTIONS: Questions 15 through 20 consist of three lines of code letters and numbers. The numbers on each line should correspond with the code letters on the same line in accordance with the table below.

Code Letter	F	X	L	M	R	W	T	S	B	H
Corresponding Number	0	1	2	3	4	5	6	7	8	9

On some of the lines, an error exists in the coding. Compare the letters and numbers in each question carefully. If you find an error or errors on
   only one of the lines in the question, mark your answer A;
   any two lines in the question, mark your answer B;
   all three lines in the question, mark your answer C;
   none of the lines in the question, mark your answer D.

SAMPLE QUESTION: LTSXHMF   2671930
                               TBRWHLM   6845913
                               SXLBFMR   5128034

In the above sample, the first line is correct since each code letter listed has the correct corresponding number. On the second line, an error exists because code letter L should have the number 2 instead of the number 1. On the third line, an error exists because the code letter S should have the number 7 instead of the number 5. Since there are errors on two of the three lines, the correct answer is B.

15. XMWBHLR   1358924
    FWSLRHX   0572491
    MTXBLTS   3618267

15._____

16. XTLSMRF   1627340
    BMHRFLT   8394026
    HLTSWRX   9267451

16._____

17. LMBSFXS   2387016   17.____
    RWLHBSX   4532871
    SMFXBHW   7301894

18. RSTWTSML   47657632   18.____
    LXRMHFBS   21439087
    FTLBMRWX   06273451

19. XSRSBWFM   17478603   19.____
    BRMXRMXT   84314216
    XSTFBWRL   17609542

20. TMSBXHLS   63781927   20.____
    RBSFLFWM   48702053
    MHFXWTRS   39015647

KEY (CORRECT ANSWERS)

1. D   11. D
2. A   12. A
3. D   13. C
4. C   14. A
5. D   15. D

6. C   16. A
7. D   17. C
8. B   18. B
9. C   19. C
10. B   20. D

EXAMINATION SECTION
TEST 1

DIRECTIONS: Each question or incomplete statement is followed by several suggested answers or completions. Select the one that BEST answers the question or completes the statement. *PRINT THE LETTER OF THE CORRECT ANSWER IN THE SPACE AT THE RIGHT.*

1. According to one suggested filing system, no more than 12 folders should be filed behind any one file guide and from 10 to 20 file guides should be used in each file drawer. Based on this filing system, the MAXIMUM number of folders that a four-drawer file cabinet can hold is

   A. 240   B. 480   C. 960   D. 1200

2. A certain office uses three different forms. Last year it used 3500 copies of Form L, 6700 copies of Form M, and 10,500 copies of Form P. This year, the office expects to decrease the use of each of these forms by 5%.
   The TOTAL number of these three forms which the office expects to use this year is

   A. 10,350   B. 16,560   C. 19,665   D. 21,735

3. The hourly rate of pay for a certain part-time employee is computed by dividing his yearly salary rate by the number of hours in the work year. The employee's yearly salary rate is $18,928, and there are 1,820 hours in the work year.
   If this employee works 18 hours during one week, his TOTAL earnings for these 18 hours are

   A. $180.00   B. $183.60   C. $187.20   D. $190.80

4. Assume that the regular work week of an employee is 35 hours and that the employee is paid for any extra hours worked according to the following schedule. For hours worked in excess of 35 hours, up to and including 40 hours, the employee receives his regular hourly rate of pay. For hours worked in excess of 40 hours, the employee receives 1 1/2 times his hourly rate of pay.
   If the employee's hourly rate of pay is $11.20 and he works 43 hours during a certain week, his TOTAL pay for the week would be

   A. $481.60   B. $498.40   C. $556.00   D. $722.40

5. The following table shows the total amount of money owed on the bills sent to each of four different accounts and the total amount of money which has been received from each of these accounts.

Name of Account	Amount Owed	Amount Received
Arnold	$55,989	$37,898
Barry	$97,276	$79,457
Carter	$62,736	$47,769
Daley	$77,463	$59,534

   The balance of an account is determined by subtracting the amount received from the amount owed. Based on this method of determining a balance, the account with the LARGEST balance is

   A. Arnold   B. Barry   C. Carter   D. Daley

6. Suppose that you are transferring the charges of a number of hospital patients from each patient's individual records to one form.
   To make sure that the amounts are transferred accurately, it would be BEST for you to

   A. check each amount copies against the appropriate patient's records after completing the transfers
   B. have someone read the amounts from the patient records while you write them on the form
   C. copy the amounts slowly and carefully so that you will not make a mistake
   D. write each amount lightly in pencil and then go over each number heavily with a pen

6.____

7. Assume that your office ordered supplies from a vendor on December 1. These supplies are to be used starting on February 2 of the following year, and it is essential that they arrive by that date.
   Of the following, which is the BEST way to assure that the supplies arrive on time?

   A. Contact the post office before February 2 and inquire about the vendor's record in shipping supplies
   B. Keep in contact with the vendor until the supplies arrive, and follow up on any problems which arise
   C. Mail a duplicate copy of the order to the vendor sometime in January to serve as a reminder
   D. Telephone the vendor a week before February 2, and ask whether the supplies were shipped

7.____

8. Assume that you are working in an admissions area of a hospital and you are completing an admissions form for a new patient. In order to complete the form, you have to obtain certain information from the patient, such as his name, address, and age, and write it on the form.
   Of the following, the FIRST action you should take after the patient tells you his name is to

   A. ask the patient for a copy of his birth certificate in order to verify his name
   B. ask the patient whether he has been a patient in your hospital before
   C. tell the patient to write his name on the form
   D. write his name in the appropriate place on the admissions form

8.____

9. Of the following, the BEST reason for a clerical division to have its own photocopying machine is that the division

   A. frequently needs copies of incoming correspondence
   B. frequently receives photographic negatives in the mail
   C. must enter the receipt date on all incoming mail
   D. uses 5,000 copies of a form each month

9.____

10. In your assignment to a hospital admitting office, you will be required to personally fill out an admissions form for each person before he is admitted to the hospital. Of the following, the MOST accurate way for you to obtain the information you need from a person is to

    A. ask him one question at a time based on the information you need
    B. ask him only those questions which can be answered by the words *yes* or *no*

10.____

C. give him the form and tell him to fill it out correctly
D. have him complete the entire form and then sign it yourself

Questions 11-20.

DIRECTIONS: Each of Questions 11 through 20 gives the identification number and name of aperson who has received treatment at a certain hospital. You are to choose the option (A, B, C, or D) which has EXACTLY the same identification number and name as those given in the question.

SAMPLE QUESTION

123765 Frank Y. Jones

A. 123675 Frank Y. Jones
B. 123765 Frank T. Jones
C. 123765 Frank Y. Johns
D. 123765 Frank Y. Jones

The correct answer is D. Only option D shows the identification number and name exactly as they are in the sample question. Option A has a mistake in the identification number. Option B has a mistake in the middle initial of the name. Option C has a mistake in the last name.

Now answer Questions 11 through 20 in the same manner.

11. 754898   Diane Malloy   11.____

   A. 745898   Diane Malloy
   B. 754898   Dion Malloy
   C. 754898   Diane Malloy
   D. 754898   Diane Maloy

12. 661018   Ferdinand Figueroa   12.____

   A. 661818   Ferdinand Figeuroa
   B. 661618   Ferdinand Figueroa
   C. 661818   Ferdnand Figueroa
   D. 661818   Ferdinand Figueroa

13. 100101   Norman D. Braustein   13.____

   A. 100101   Norman D. Braustein
   B. 101001   Norman D. Braustein
   C. 100101   Norman P. Braustien
   D. 100101   Norman D. Bruastein

14. 838696   Robert Kittredge   14.____

   A. 838969   Robert Kittredge
   B. 838696   Robert Kittredge
   C. 388696   Robert Kittredge
   D. 838696   Robert Kittridge

15. 243716   Abraham Soletsky   15.____

    A. 243716   Abrahm Soletsky
    B. 243716   Abraham Solestky
    C. 243176   Abraham Soletsky
    D. 243716   Abraham Soletsky

16. 981121   Phillip M. Maas   16.____

    A. 981121   Phillip M. Mass
    B. 981211   Phillip M. Maas
    C. 981121   Phillip M. Maas
    D. 981121   Phillip N. Maas

17. 786556   George Macalusso   17.____

    A. 785656   George Macalusso
    B. 786556   George Macalusso
    C. 786556   George Maculasso
    D. 786556   George Macluasso

18. 639472   Eugene Weber   18.____

    A. 639472   Eugene Weber
    B. 639472   Eugene Webre
    C. 693472   Eugene Weber
    D. 639742   Eugene Weber

19. 724936   John J. Lomonaco   19.____

    A. 724936   John J. Lomanoco
    B. 724396   John J. Lomonaco
    C. 724936   John J. Lomonaco
    D. 724936   John J. Lamonaco

20. 899868   Michael Schnitzer   20.____

    A. 899868   Micheal Schnitzer
    B. 898968   Michael Schnizter
    C. 899688   Michael Schnitzer
    D. 899868   Michael Schnitzer

KEY (CORRECT ANSWERS)

1.	C	11.	C
2.	C	12.	D
3.	C	13.	A
4.	B	14.	B
5.	A	15.	D
6.	A	16.	C
7.	A	17.	B
8.	D	18.	A
9.	A	19.	C
10.	A	20.	D

TEST 2

DIRECTIONS: Each question or incomplete statement is followed by several suggested answers or completions. Select the one that BEST answers the question or completes the statement. *PRINT THE LETTER OF TEE CORRECT ANSWER IN THE SPACE AT THE RIGHT.*

Questions 1-10.

DIRECTIONS: Questions 1 through 10 are to be answered on the basis of the information and the form given below.

The form below is a Daily Summary of Clinic Visits and lists ten persons who used a clinic in Washington Hospital on September 4.

The form includes the following information about each patient: Name, identification number, date of birth, case number, fee, and bill number.

| SEPTEMBER 4 WASHINGTON HOSPITAL - DAILY SUMMARY OF CLINIC VISITS ||||||||
| Name of Patient Last, First | Identification Number | Date of Birth ||| Case Number | Fee | Bill Number |
		Mo.	Day	Yr.			
Enders, John	89-4143-67	08	01	71	434317	$ 90.00	129631
Dawes, Mary	71-6142-69	11	17	66	187963	$ 47.50	129632
Lang, Donald	54-1213-73	10	07	75	897436	$180.00	129633
Eiger, Alan	18-7649-63	06	19	51	134003	$110.00	129634
Ramirez, Jose	61-4319-69	03	30	96	379030	$130.00	129635
Ilono, Frank	13-9161-57	08	19	83	565645	$ 66.00	129636
Sloan, Irene	55-8643-66	05	13	57	799732	$112.50	129637
Long, Thomas	41-3963-74	12	03	76	009784	$ 37.50	129638
McKay, Cathy	14-9633-44	05	09	66	000162	$ 96.00	129639
Dale, Sarah	86-1113-69	11	13	59	543211	$138.00	129640

1. The fee for Cathy McKay is LESS than the fee for

   A. John Enders B. Alan Eiger
   C. Frank Ilono D. Thomas Long

   1.____

2. The two patients who were born in the same year are

   A. John Enders and Frank Ilono
   B. Mary Dawes and Sarah Dale
   C. Donald Lang and Thomas Long
   D. Cathy McKay and Mary Dawes

   2.____

3. The case number of Irene Sloan is

   A. 979732 B. 799372 C. 799732 D. 797732

   3.____

4. Cathy McKay's identification number is

   A. 44-9633-14 B. 14-9633-44
   C. 000162   D. 129639

   4.____

5. Frank Ilono's case number is 5.____

   A. 556645   B. 565465   C. 565645   D. 565654

6. The bill numbers for Jose Ramirez and Thomas Long are 6.____

   A. 129635 and 129638
   B. 129635 and 129683
   C. 129634 and 129638
   D. 129634 and 129637

7. The fees for Donald Lang, Sarah Dale, and Mary Dawes are 7.____

   A. $47.50, $180.00, and $96.00
   B. $110.00, $138.00, and $90.00
   C. $180.00, $130.00, and $47.50
   D. $180.00, $138.00, and $47.50

8. The case numbers for Thomas Long and Mary Dawes are 8.____

   A. 009784 and 187963
   B. 090784 and 187963
   C. 009784 and 187693
   D. 009874 and 187963

9. The identification numbers for Frank Ilono and Donald Lang are 9.____

   A. 13-9161-57 and 54-1312-73
   B. 54-1213-73 and 13-6191-57
   C. 13-9161-57 and 54-1213-73
   D. 54-1213-37 and 13-9161-57

10. The birth dates of Irene Sloan, John Enders, and Sarah Dale are 10.____

    A. 05/31/57, 01/08/71, and 11/13/69
    B. 05/13/67, 08/01/71, and 11/13/69
    C. 05/31/57, 01/08/71, and 11/13/59
    D. 05/13/57, 08/01/71, and 11/13/59

Questions 11-15.

DIRECTIONS: Questions 11 through 15 consist of sets of names and addresses. In each question, the name and address in Column II should be an EXACT copy of the name and address in Column I. Compare the name and address in Column II with the name and address in Column I.

If there is an error in the name only, mark your answer A;
If there is an error in the address only, mark your answer B;
If there is an error in both the name and address, mark your answer C;
If there is NO error in either the name or address, mark your answer D.

SAMPLE QUESTION

COLUMN I	COLUMN II
Mildred Bonilla	Mildred Bonila
511 West 186 Street	511 West 186 Street
New York, N.Y. 10033	New York, N.Y. 10032

Compare the name and address in Column II with the name and address in Column I. The name Bonila in Column II is spelled Bonilla in Column I. The zip code 10032 in Column II is given as 10033 in Column I. Since there is an error in both the name and address, the answer to the sample question is C.

Now answer Questions 11 through 15 in the same manner.

COLUMN I | COLUMN II

11. Mr. & Mrs. George Petersson
    87-11 91st Avenue
    Woodhaven, New York 11421

    Mr. & Mrs. George Peterson
    87-11 91st Avenue
    Woodhaven, New York 11421

    11.____

12. Mr. Ivan Klebnikov
    1848 Newkirk Avenue
    Brooklyn, New York 11226

    Mr. Ivan Klebikov
    1848 Newkirk Avenue
    Brooklyn, New York 11622

    12.____

13. Samuel Rothfleisch
    71 Pine Street
    New York, New York 10005

    Samuel Rothfleisch
    71 Pine Street
    New York, New York 10005

    13.____

14. Mrs. Isabel Tonnessen
    198 East 185th Street
    Bronx, New York 10458

    Mrs. Isabel Tonnessen
    189 East 185th Street
    Bronx, New York 10458

    14.____

15. Esteban Perez
    173 Eighth Street
    Staten Island, N.Y. 10306

    Estaban Perez
    173 Eighth Street
    Staten Island, N.Y. 10306

    15.____

16. The MAIN purpose of an invoice is to   16.____

    A. confirm receipt of an order
    B. list items being sent to a buyer
    C. order items from a company
    D. provide written proof that a shipment has been received

17. You have been told to add various amounts listed on a billing form by operating a calcu-   17.____
    lating machine. The machine prints on a roll of paper tape all amounts added and the answer to the computation.
    Of the following, the LEAST appropriate use for this tape is to

    A. check that no amounts were left out during the computation
    B. check that the amounts were entered correctly into the machine
    C. keep a record of the computation
    D. prove that the amounts on the original document are correct

18. Assume that you are working in a storehouse of a hospital system. One of your tasks is   18.____
    to fill requisitions from hospitals for office supplies. When a requisition is received, you much check inventory cards to determine whether an item is available. One day, you receive a requisition for office supplies; and upon checking the inventory cards, you find that one of the items ordered, a particular kind of paper, is not available. However, the other items are ready for shipment to the hospital. Of the following, the BEST course of action for you to take in this situation is to

A. have those items which are available sent to the hospital with an indication of which items were sent
B. purchase the missing paper yourself and then have the complete order sent to the hospital
C. substitute any other paper which is available and then have the order sent to the hospital
D. wait until the missing paper is available and then have the complete order sent to the hospital

19. One of your duties is to get certain information from people who are being treated at a hospital clinic. One day, you are trying to get this information from a person who begins to talk about matters unrelated to the information you are trying to obtain.
Of the following, the BEST course of action for you to take in this situation is to

    A. allow the individual to continue talking about the unrelated matters since he will probably return to the information you need in a short time
    B. ask the individual a question that may lead him back to the information you need
    C. end the interview and obtain the information from other sources
    D. tell the individual to give you the information you need and not discuss the unrelated matters

19._____

20. You have just asked a patient a question about the kind of hospitalization insurance he has.
The BEST way for you to make sure that you understand his answer to the question is to

    A. ask the question again in a slightly different way and see if you get approximately the same answer
    B. ask the same question again and listen carefully to see if the answer is the same
    C. repeat the answer in your own words and ask the patient if that is what he meant
    D. write the answer down on a piece of paper and read it back to the patient

20._____

KEY (CORRECT ANSWERS)

1. B
2. D
3. C
4. B
5. C

6. A
7. D
8. A
9. C
10. D

11. A
12. C
13. D
14. B
15. A

16. B
17. D
18. A
19. B
20. C

EXAMINATION SECTION
TEST 1

DIRECTIONS: Each question or incomplete statement is followed by several suggested answers or completions. Select the one that BEST answers the question or completes the statement. *PRINT THE LETTER OF THE CORRECT ANSWER IN THE SPACE AT THE RIGHT.*

Questions 1-10.

DIRECTIONS: Questions 1 through 10 consist of four names each. In the space at the right, print the letter of the name which should be filed FIRST according to generally accepted alphabetic filing rules.

1. A. George St. John B. Thomas Santos 1.____
   C. Frances Starks D. Mary S. Stranum

2. A. Franklin Carrol B. Timothy Carrol 2.____
   C. Timothy S. Carol D. Timothy S. Carol

3. A. Christie-Barry Storage 3.____
   B. John Christie-Barry
   C. The Christie-Barry Company
   D. Anne Christie-Barrie

4. A. Inter State Travel Co. B. Interstate Car Rental 4.____
   C. Inter State Trucking D. Interstate Lending Inst.

5. A. The Los Angeles Tile Co. 5.____
   B. Anita F. Los
   C. The Lost & Found Detective Agency
   D. Jason Los-Brio

6. A. Prince Charles B. Prince Charles Coiffures 6.____
   C. Chas. F. Prince D. Thomas A. Charles

7. A. U.S. Dept. of Agriculture B. United States Aircraft Co. 7.____
   C. U.S. Air Transport, Inc. D. The United Union

8. A. Meyer's Art Shop B. Frank B. Meyer 8.____
   C. Meyers' Paint Store D. Meyer and Goldberg

9. A. David Des Laurier B. Des Moines Flower Shop 9.____
   C. Henry Desanto D. Mary L. Desta

10. A. Jeffrey Van Der Meer B. Jeffrey M. Vander 10.____
    C. Jeffrey Van D. Wallace Meer

Questions 11-20.

DIRECTIONS: Questions 11 through 20 are to be answered on the basis of the following instructions: For each such numbered set of names, addresses, and numbers listed in Columns I and II, select your answer from the following options:

93

2 (#1)

A. The names in Columns I and II are different.
B. The addresses in Columns I and II are different.
C. The numbers in Columns I and II are different.
D. The names, addresses, and numbers in Columns I and II are identical.

COLUMN I	COLUMN II	
11. Francis Jones 62 Stately Avenue 96-12446	Francis Jones 62 Stately Avenue 96-21446	11.___
12. Julio Montez 19 Ponderosa Road 56-73161	Julio Montez 19 Ponderosa Road 56-71361	12.___
13. Mary Mitchell 2314 Melbourne Drive 68-92172	Mary Mitchell 2314 Melbourne Drive 68-92172	13.___
14. Harry Patterson 25 Dunne Street 14-33430	Harry Patterson 25 Dunne Street 14-34330	14.___
15. Patrick Murphy 171 West Hosmer Street 93-81214	Patrick Murphy 171 West Hosmer Street 93-18214	15.___
16. August Schultz 816 St. Clair Avenue 53-40149	August Schultz 816 St. Claire Avenue 53-40149	16.___
17. George Taft 72 Runnymede Street 47-04033	George Taft 72 Runnymede Street 47-04023	17.___
18. Angus Henderson 1418 Madison Street 81-76375	Angus Henderson 1418 Madison Street 81-76375	18.___
19. Carolyn Mazur 12 Riverview Road 38-99615	Carolyn Mazur 12 Rivervane Road 38-99615	19.___
20. Adele Russell 1725 Lansing Lane 72-91962	Adela Russell 1725 Lansing Lane 72-91962	20.___

21. The reason why the analysis of mortality statistics is an IMPORTANT tool of modern public health administration is that it

    A. provides a measure of the state of health of the people of the city
    B. provides for personal records of births and deaths
    C. indicates need for methods of disposition of human remains
    D. provides a method of uncovering changes in birth or death certificates

22. When a fetal death occurs in a hospital, it should be reported to the Health Department PRIMARILY by the

    A. person in charge at the hospital
    B. attending nurse
    C. person in charge of the maternity clinic with which the attending physician or midwife is associated
    D. chief medical examiner

23. When a nurse midwife attends at or after a fetal death in a location other than a hospital, she SHOULD

    A. sign the certificate of fetal death after it has been prepared by the physician, and forward it
    B. prepare the certificate of fetal death and confidential medical report and have it examined and countersigned by a physician before forwarding it
    C. prepare the certificate of fetal death and forward it thereafter to the nearest hospital
    D. prepare the certificate of fetal death and forward it thereafter to the commissioner of health

24. According to the Health Code, which of the following next-of-kin should be notified of an adult death FIRST?

    A. Parents of deceased
    B. Spouse of deceased
    C. Children of deceased who are over 21
    D. Attorney of record

25. A registry of deaths shall be maintained and permanently preserved in each hospital. When a death occurs in a hospital, the person RESPONSIBLE for entering the death in the registry shall be

    A. the floor nursing supervisor
    B. the medical superintendent on duty
    C. any licensed physician
    D. the person who prepares the death certificate

26. The name below that would MOST likely need to be cross-referenced in an alphabetic filing system is

    A. Dr. George G. D'Arcy
    B. Mrs. Dorothy C. Crown
    C. Mr. David E. Forbes-Watkins
    D. Prof. Harry D. Van Tassell

Questions 27-30.

DIRECTIONS: Questions 27 through 30 refer to the following Certificate of Death index number: 156-74-200863.

27. The numerical component that indicates the CITY in which death occurred is　　27.___
    A. 200　　　　B. 156　　　　C. 863　　　　D. 74

28. The numerical component that indicates the CASE NUMBER is　　28.___
    A. 00863　　　B. 200863　　　C. 156-74　　　D. 74-200863

29. The numerical component that indicates the BOROUGH in which death occurred is　　29.___
    A. 1　　　　　B. 2　　　　　C. 3　　　　　D. 4

30. This Certificate of Death INDEX NUMBER refers to a death that occurred in　　30.___
    A. the Bronx　　　　　　　　B. Queens
    C. Brooklyn　　　　　　　　　D. Staten Island

KEY (CORRECT ANSWERS)

1.	A	16.	B
2.	C	17.	C
3.	D	18.	A
4.	B	19.	B
5.	B	20.	A
6.	D	21.	A
7.	C	22.	A
8.	A	23.	B
9.	C	24.	B
10.	D	25.	D
11.	C	26.	C
12.	C	27.	B
13.	D	28.	A
14.	C	29.	B
15.	C	30.	A

EXAMINATION SECTION
TEST 1

DIRECTIONS: Each question or incomplete statement is followed by several suggested answers or completions. Select the one that BEST answers the question or completes the statement. *PRINT THE LETTER OF THE CORRECT ANSWER IN THE SPACE AT THE RIGHT.*

Questions 1-20.

DIRECTIONS: Column I below lists words used in medical practice. Column II lists phrases which describe the words in Column I. Opposite the number preceding each of the words in Column I, place the letter preceding the phrase in Column II which BEST describes the word in Column I.

COLUMN I

1. Abrasion
2. Aseptic
3. Cardiac
4. Catarrh
5. Contamination
6. Dermatology
7. Disinfectant
8. Dyspepsia
9. Epidemic
10. Epidermis
11. Incubation
12. Microscope
13. Pediatrics
14. Plasma
15. Prenatal
16. Retina
17. Syphilis
18. Syringe
19. Toxemia
20. Vaccine

COLUMN II

A. A disturbance of digestion
B. Destroying the germs of disease
C. A general poisoning of the blood
D. An instrument used for injecting fluids
E. A scraping off of the skin
F. Free from disease germs
G. An apparatus for viewing internal organs by means of x-rays
H. An instrument for assisting the eye in observing minute objects
I. An inoculable immunizing agent
J. The extensive prevalence in a community of a
K. Chemical product of an organ
L. Preceding birth
M. Fever
N. The branch of medical science that relates to the skin and its diseases
O. Fluid part of the blood
P. The science of the hygienic care of children
Q. Infection by contact
R. Relating to the heart
S. Inner structure of the eye
T. Outer portion of the skin
U. Pertaining to the ductless glands
V. An infectious venereal disease
W. The development of an infectious disease from the period of infection to that of the appearance of the first symptoms
X. Simple inflammation of a mucous membrane
Y. An instrument for measuring blood pressure

1._____
2._____
3._____
4._____
5._____
6._____
7._____
8._____
9._____
10._____
11._____
12._____
13._____
14._____
15._____
16._____
17._____
18._____
19._____
20._____

Questions 21-25.

DIRECTIONS: Each of Questions 21 through 25 consists of four words. Three of these words belong together. One word does NOT belong with the other three. For each group of words, you are to select the one word which does NOT belong with the other three words.

21. A. conclude B. terminate C. initiate D. end 21.___

22. A. deficient B. inadequate 22.___
    C. excessive D. insufficient

23. A. rare B. unique C. unusual D. frequent 23.___

24. A. unquestionable B. uncertain 24.___
    C. doubtful D. indefinite

25. A. stretch B. contract C. extend D. expand 25.___

KEY (CORRECT ANSWERS)

1. E
2. F
3. R
4. X
5. Q

6. N
7. B
8. A
9. J
10. T

11. W
12. H
13. P
14. O
15. L

16. S
17. V
18. D
19. C
20. I

21. C
22. C
23. D
24. A
25. B

TEST 2

DIRECTIONS: Each question or incomplete statement is followed by several suggested answers or completions. Select the one that BEST answers the question or completes the statement. *PRINT THE LETTER OF THE CORRECT ANSWER IN THE SPACE AT THE RIGHT.*

Questions 1-4.

DIRECTIONS: Questions 1 through 4 pertain to the meaning of terms which may be encountered in laboratory work. For each question, select the option whose meaning is MOST NEARLY the same as that of the numbered item.

1. Atrophied   1._____

   A. enlarged
   B. relaxed
   C. strengthened
   D. wasted

2. Leucocyte   2._____

   A. white cell
   B. red cell
   C. epithelial cell
   D. dermal cell

3. Permeable   3._____

   A. volatile
   B. variable
   C. flexible
   D. penetrable

4. Attenuate   4._____

   A. dilute
   B. infect
   C. oxidize
   D. strengthen

Questions 5-11.

DIRECTIONS: For Questions 5 through 11, select the letter preceding the word which means MOST NEARLY the same as the first word.

5. legible   5._____

   A. readable   B. eligible   C. learned   D. lawful

6. observe   6._____

   A. assist   B. watch   C. correct   D. oppose

7. habitual   7._____

   A. punctual
   B. occasional
   C. usual
   D. actual

8. chronological   8._____

   A. successive
   B. earlier
   C. later
   D. studious

9. arrest
   A. punish   B. run   C. threaten   D. stop

10. abstain
    A. refrain   B. indulge   C. discolor   D. spoil

11. toxic
    A. poisonous   B. decaying
    C. taxing   D. defective

12. The *initial* contact is of great importance in setting a pattern for future relations.
    The word *initial*, as used in this sentence, means MOST NEARLY
    A. first   B. written   C. direct   D. hidden

13. The doctor prescribed a diet which was *adequate* for the patient's needs.
    The word *adequate*, as used in this sentence, means MOST NEARLY
    A. insufficient   B. unusual
    C. required   D. enough

14. The child was reported to be suffering from a vitamin *deficiency*.
    The word *deficiency*, as used in this sentence, means MOST NEARLY
    A. surplus   B. infection   C. shortage   D. injury

15. In obtaining medical case data, a medical record librarian should discourage the patient from giving *irrelevant* information.
    The word *irrelevant*, as used in this sentence, means MOST NEARLY
    A. too detailed   B. pertaining to relatives
    C. insufficient   D. inappropriate

16. The doctor requested that a *tentative* appointment be made for the patient.
    The word *tentative*, as used in this sentence, means MOST NEARLY
    A. definite   B. subject to change
    C. later   D. of short duration

17. The black plague resulted in an usually high *mortality rate* in the population of Europe.
    The term *mortality rate*, as used in this sentence, means MOST NEARLY
    A. future immunity of the people
    B. death rate
    C. general weakening of the health of the people
    D. sickness rate

18. The public health assistant was asked to file a number of *identical* reports on the case.
    The word *identical*, as used in this sentence, means MOST NEARLY
    A. accurate   B. detailed   C. same   D. different

19. The nurse assisted in *the biopsy* of the patient.
    The word *biopsy*, as used in this sentence, means MOST NEARLY

    A. autopsy
    B. excision and diagnostic study of tissue
    C. biography and health history
    D. administering of anesthesia

    19.____

20. The assistant noted that the swelling on the patient's face had *subsided*.
    The word *subsided*, as used in this sentence, means MOST NEARLY

    A. become aggravated   B. increased
    C. vanished   D. abated

    20.____

21. The patient was given food *intravenously*.
    The word *intravenously*, as used in this sentence, means MOST NEARLY

    A. orally   B. against his will
    C. through the veins   D. without condiment

    21.____

Questions 22-25.

DIRECTIONS: Each of Questions 22 through 25 consists of four words. Three of these words belong together. One word does NOT belong with the other three. For each group of words, you are to select the one word which does NOT belong with the other three words.

22.	A. accelerate	B. quicken	C. accept	D. hasten		22.____
23.	A. sever	B. rupture	C. rectify	D. tear		23.____
24.	A. innocuous	B. injurious	C. dangerous	D. harmful		24.____
25.	A. adulterate		B. contaminate			25.____
	C. taint		D. disinfect			

KEY (CORRECT ANSWERS)

1. D   11. A   21. C
2. A   12. A   22. C
3. D   13. D   23. C
4. A   14. C   24. A
5. A   15. D   25. D

6. B   16. B
7. C   17. B
8. A   18. C
9. D   19. B
10. A   20. D

TEST 3

DIRECTIONS: Each question or incomplete statement is followed by several suggested answers or completions. Select the one that BEST answers the question or completes the statement. *PRINT THE LETTER OF THE CORRECT ANSWER IN THE SPACE AT THE RIGHT.*

Questions 1-25.

DIRECTIONS: Each of Questions 1 through 25 consists of a word, in capitals, followed by four suggested meanings of the word. For each question, indicate in the space at the right the letter preceding the word which means MOST NEARLY the same as the word in capitals.

1. TEMPORARY
   - A. permanently
   - B. for a limited time
   - C. at the same time
   - D. frequently

2. INQUIRE
   - A. order
   - B. agree
   - C. ask
   - D. discharge

3. SUFFICIENT
   - A. enough
   - B. inadequate
   - C. thorough
   - D. capable

4. AMBULATORY
   - A. bedridden
   - B. left-handed
   - C. walking
   - D. laboratory

5. DILATE
   - A. enlarge
   - B. contract
   - C. revise
   - D. restrict

6. NUTRITIOUS
   - A. protective
   - B. healthful
   - C. fattening
   - D. nourishing

7. CONGENITAL
   - A. with pleasure
   - B. defective
   - C. likeable
   - D. existing from birth

8. ISOLATION
   - A. sanitation
   - B. quarantine
   - C. rudeness
   - D. exposure

9. SPASM
   - A. splash
   - B. twitch
   - C. space
   - D. blow

10. HEMORRHAGE

    A. bleeding
    B. ulcer
    C. hereditary disease
    D. lack of blood

11. NOXIOUS

    A. gaseous   B. harmful   C. soothing   D. repulsive

12. PYOGENIC

    A. disease producing
    B. fever producing
    C. pus forming
    D. water forming

13. RENAL

    A. brain   B. heart   C. kidney   D. stomach

14. ENDEMIC

    A. epidemic
    B. endermic
    C. endoblast
    D. peculiar to a particular people or locality, as a disease

15. MACULATION

    A. reticulation
    B. inoculation
    C. maturation
    D. defilement

16. TOLERATE

    A. fear   B. forgive   C. allow   D. despise

17. VENTILATE

    A. vacate   B. air   C. extricate   D. heat

18. SUPERIOR

    A. perfect
    B. subordinate
    C. lower
    D. higher

19. EXTREMITY

    A. extent   B. limb   C. illness   D. execution

20. DIVULGED

    A. unrefined   B. secreted   C. revealed   D. divided

21. SIPHON

    A. drain   B. drink   C. compute   D. discard

22. EXPIRATION

    A. trip
    B. demonstration
    C. examination
    D. end

23. AEROSOL 23.____

    A. a gas dispersed in a liquid
    B. a liquid dispersed in a gas
    C. a liquid dispersed in a solid
    D. a solid dispersed in a liquid

24. ETIOLOGY 24.____

    A. cause of a disease   B. method of cure
    C. method of diagnosis   D. study of insects

25. IN VITRO 25.____

    A. in alkali   B. in the body
    C. in the test tube   D. in vacuum

KEY (CORRECT ANSWERS)

1.	B	11.	B
2.	C	12.	C
3.	A	13.	C
4.	C	14.	D
5.	A	15.	D
6.	D	16.	C
7.	D	17.	B
8.	B	18.	D
9.	B	19.	B
10.	A	20.	C

21. A
22. D
23. B
24. A
25. C

NAME AND NUMBER CHECKING
EXAMINATION SECTION
TEST 1

DIRECTIONS: This test is designed to measure your speed/and accuracy. You are urged to work both quickly and accurately and to do correctly as many lists as you can in the time allowed. The test consists of lists or pairs of names and numbers. Count the number of IDENTICAL pairs in each list. Then, select the correct number, 1, 2, 3, 4, 5, and indicate your choice in the space at the right. Two sample questions are presented for your guidance, together with the correct solutions.

<u>SAMPLE LIST A</u>
Adelphi College	– Adelphia College
Braxton Corp	– Braxeton Corp.
Wassaic State School	– Wassaic State School
Central Islip State Hospital	– Central Isllip State Hospital
Greenwich House	– Greenwich House

NOTE: There are only two correct pairs—Wassaic State School and Greenwich House. Therefore, the CORRECT answer is 2.

<u>SAMPLE LIST B</u>
78453694	– 78453684
784530	– 784530
533	– 534
67845	– 67845
2368745	– 2368755

NOTE: There are only two correct pairs—784530 and 67845. Therefore, the CORRECT answer is 2.

<u>LIST 1</u>   1.____
98654327	- 98654327
74932564	- 7492564
61438652	- 61438652
01297653	- 01287653
1865439765	- 1865439765

<u>LIST 2</u>   2.____
478362	- 478363
278354792	- 278354772
9327	- 9327
297384625	- 27384625
6428156	- 6428158

LIST 3   3.____
    Abbey House   - Abbey House
    Actor's Fund Home   - Actor's Fund Home
    Adrian Memorial   - Adrian Memorial
    A. Clayton Powell Home   - Clayton Powell House
    Abbot E. Kittredge Club   - Abbott E. Kitteredge Club

LIST 4   4.____
    3682   - 3692
    21937453829   - 31927453829
    723   - 733
    2763920   - 2763920
    47293   - 47293

LIST 5   5.____
    Adra House   - Adra House
    Adolescents' Court   - Adolescents' Court
    Cliff Villa   - Cliff Villa
    Clark Neighborhood House - Clark Neighborhood House
    Alma Mathews House   - Alma Mathews House

LIST 6   6.____
    28734291   - 28734271
    63810263849   - 63810263846
    26831027   - 26831027
    368291   - 368291
    7238102637   - 7238102637

LIST 7   7.____
    Albion State T.S.   - Albion State T.C.
    Clara de Hirsch Home   - Clara De Hirsch Home
    Alice Carrington Royce   - Alice Carington Royce
    Alice Chopin Nursery   - Alice Chapin Nursery
    Lighthouse Eye Clinic   - Lighthouse Eye Clinic

LIST 8   8.____
    327   - 329
    712438291026   - 712438291026
    2753829142   - 275382942
    826287   - 826289
    26435162839   - 26435162839

LIST 9   9.____
    Letchworth Village   - Letchworth Village
    A.A.A.E. Inc.   - A.A.A.E. Inc.
    Clear Pool Camp   - Clear Pool Camp
    A.M.M.L.A. Inc.   - A.M.M.L.A. Inc.
    J.G. Harbard   - J.G. Harbord

3 (#1)

LIST 10   10.____
    8254　　　　　　　　　　- 8256
    2641526　　　　　　　　- 2641526
    4126389012　　　　　　- 4126389102
    725　　　　　　　　　　- 725
    76253917287　　　　　　- 76253917287

LIST 11   11.____
    Attica State Prison　　　- Attica State Prison
    Nellie Murrah　　　　　　- Nellie Murrah
    Club Marshall　　　　　　- Club Marshal
    Assissium Casea-Maria　- Assissium Casa-Maria
    The Homestead　　　　　- The Homestead

LIST 12   12.____
    2691　　　　　　　　　　- 2691
    623819253627　　　　　- 623819253629
    28637　　　　　　　　　- 28937
    278392736　　　　　　　- 278392736
    52739　　　　　　　　　- 52739

LIST 13   13.____
    A.I.C.P. Boys Camp　　　- A.I.C.P. Boy's Camp
    Einar Chrystie　　　　　　- Einar Christyie
    Astoria Center　　　　　　- Astoria Center
    G. Frederick Brown　　　- G. Federick Browne
    Vacation Service　　　　　- Vacation Services

LIST 14   14.____
    728352689　　　　　　　- 728352688
    643728　　　　　　　　　- 643728
    37829176　　　　　　　　- 37827196
    8425367　　　　　　　　　- 8425369
    65382018　　　　　　　　- 65382018

LIST 15   15.____
    E.S. Streim　　　　　　　- E.S. Strim
    Charles E. Higgins　　　　- Charles E. Higgins
    Baluvelt, N.Y.　　　　　　- Blauwelt, N.Y.
    Roberta Magdalen　　　- Roberto Magdalen
    Ballard School　　　　　　- Ballard School

LIST 16   16.____
    7382　　　　　　　　　　- 7392
    281374538299　　　　　- 291374538299
    623　　　　　　　　　　　- 633
    6273730　　　　　　　　　- 6273730
    63392　　　　　　　　　　- 63392

LIST 17
- Orrin Otis — - Orrin Otis
- Barat Settlement — - Barat Settlemen
- Emmanuel House — - Emmanuel House
- William T. McCreery — - William T. McCreery
- Seamen's Home — - Seaman's Home

17.____

LIST 18
- 72824391 — - 72834371
- 3729106237 — - 37291106237
- 82620163849 — - 82620163846
- 37638921 — - 37638921
- 82631027 — - 82631027

18.____

LIST 19
- Commonwealth Fund — - Commonwealth Fund
- Anne Johnsen — - Anne Johnson
- Bide-A-Wee Home — - Bide-a-Wee Home
- Riverdale-on-Hudson — - Riverdal-on-Hudson
- Bialystoker Home — - Bailystoker Home

19.____

LIST 20
- 9271 — - 9271
- 392918352627 — - 392018852629
- 72637 — - 72637
- 927392736 — - 927392736
- 92739 — - 92739

20.____

LIST 21
- Charles M. Stump — - Charles M. Stump
- Bourne Workshop — - Buorne Workshop
- B'nai Bi'rith — - B'nai Brith
- Poppenhuesen Institute — - Poppenheusen Institute
- Consular Service — - Consular Service

21.____

LIST 22
- 927352689 — - 927352688
- 647382 — - 648382
- 93729176 — - 93727196
- 649536718 — - 649536718
- 5835367 — - 5835369

22.____

LIST 23
- L.S. Bestend — - L.S. Bestent
- Hirsch Mfg. Co. — - Hircsh Mfg. Co.
- F.H. Storrs — - F.P. Storrs
- Camp Wassaic — - Camp Wassaic
- George Ballingham — - George Ballingham

23.____

5 (#1)

LIST 24   24.____

    372846392048   - 372846392048
    334   - 334
    7283524678   - 7283524678
    7283   - 7283
    7283629372   - 7283629372

LIST 25   25.____

    Dr. Stiles Company   - Dr. Stills Company
    Frances Hunsdon   - Frances Hunsdon
    Northrop Barrert   - Nothrup Barrent
    J.D. Brunjes   - J.D. Brunjes
    Theo. Claudel & Co.   - Theo. Claudel co.

KEY (CORRECT ANSWERS)

1.	3		11.	3
2.	1		12.	3
3.	2		13.	1
4.	2		14.	2
5.	5		15.	2
6.	3		16.	2
7.	1		17.	3
8.	2		18.	2
9.	4		19.	2
10.	3		20.	4

21. 2
22. 1
23. 2
24. 5
25. 2

TEST 2

DIRECTIONS: This test is designed to measure your speed/and accuracy. You are urged to work both quickly and accurately and to do correctly as many lists as you can in the time allowed. The test consists of lists or pairs of names and numbers. Count the number of IDENTICAL pairs in each list. Then, select the correct number, 1, 2, 3, 4, 5, and indicate your choice in the space at the right.

LIST 1 1.____
    82728   - 82738
    82736292637   - 82736292639
    728   - 738
    83926192527   - 83726192529
    82736272   - 82736272

LIST 2 2.____
    L. Pietri   - L. Pietri
    Mathewson, L.F.   - Mathewson, L.F.
    Funk & Wagnall   - Funk & Wagnalls
    Shimizu, Sojio   - Shimizu, Sojio
    Filing Equipment Bureau   - Filing Equipment Buraeu

LIST 3 3.____
    63801829374   - 63801839474
    283577657   - 283577657
    65689   - 65689
    3457892026   - 3547893026
    2779   - 2778

LIST 4 4.____
    August Caille   - August Caille
    The Well-Fare Service   - The Wel-Fare Service
    K.L.M. Process co.   - R.L.M. Process Co.
    Merrill Littell   - Merrill Littell
    Dodd & Sons   - Dodd & Son

LIST 5 5.____
    998745732   - 998745733
    723   - 723
    463849102983   - 463849102983
    8570   - 8570
    279012   - 279012

LIST 6 6.____
    M.A. Wender   - M.A. Winder
    Minneapolis Supply Co.   - Minneapolis Supply Co.
    Beverly Hills Corp   - Beverley Hills Corp.
    Trafalgar Square   - Trafalgar Square
    Phifer, D.T.   - Phiefer, D.T.

2 (#2)

LIST 7
    7834629   - 7834629
    3549806746   - 3549806746
    97802564   - 97892564
    689246   - 688246
    2578024683   - 2578024683

7.____

LIST 8
    Scadrons'   - Scadrons'
    Gensen & Bro.   - Genson & Bro.
    Firestone Co.   - Firestone Co.
    H.L. Eklund   - H.L. Eklund
    Oleomargarine Co. - Oleomargarine Co.

8.____

LIST 9
    782039485618   - 782039485618
    53829172639   - 63829172639
    892   - 892
    82937482   - 829374820
    52937456   - 53937456

9.____

LIST 10
    First Nat'l Bank   - First Nat'l Bank
    Sedgwick Machine Works - Sedgewick Machine Works
    Hectographia Co.   - Hectographia Corp.
    Levet Bros.   - Levet Bros.
    Multistamp Co., Inc. - Multistamp Co., Inc.

10.____

LIST 11
    7293   - 7293
    6382910293   - 6382910292
    981928374012   - 981928374912
    58293   - 58393
    18203649271   - 283019283745

11.____

LIST 12
    Lowrey Lb'r Co.   - Lowrey Lb'r Co.
    Fidelity Service   - Fidelity Service
    Reumann, J.A.   - Reumann, J.A.
    Duophoto Ltd.   - Duophotos Ltd.
    John Jarratt   - John Jaratt

12.____

LIST 13
    6820384   - 6820384
    383019283745   - 383019283745
    63927102   - 63928102
    91029354829   - 91029354829
    58291728   - 58291728

13.____

LIST 14
    Standard Press Co.   - Standard Press Co.
    Reliant Mf'g. Co.   - Relant Mf'g Co.
    M.C. Lynn   - M.C. Lynn
    J. Fredericks Company   - G. Fredericks Company
    Wandermann, B.S.   - Wanderman, B.S.

14.____

LIST 15
    4283910293   - 4283010203
    992018273648   - 992018273848
    620   - 629
    752937273   - 752937373
    5392   - 5392

15.____

LIST 16
    Waldorf Hotel   - Waldorf Hotel
    Aaron Machinery Co.   - Aaron Machinery Co.
    Caroline Ann Locke   - Caroline Ane Locke
    McCabe Mfg. Co.   - McCabe Mfg. Co.
    R.L. Landres   - R.L. Landers

16.____

LIST 17
    68391028364   - 68391028394
    68293   - 68293
    739201   - 739201
    72839201   - 72839211
    739917   - 739719

17.____

LIST 18
    Balsam M.M.   - Balsamm, M.M.
    Steinway & Co.   - Stienway & M. Co.
    Eugene Elliott   - Eugene A. Elliott
    Leonard Loan Co.   - Leonard Loan Co.
    Frederick Morgan   - Frederick Morgen

18.____

LIST 19
    8929   - 9820
    392836472829   - 392836572829
    462   - 4622039271
    827   - 2039276837
    53829   - 54829

19.____

LIST 20
    Danielson's Hofbrau   - Danielson's Hafbrau
    Edward A. Truarme   - Edward A. Truame
    Insulite Co.   - Insulite Co.
    Reisler Shoe Corp.   - Rielser Shoe Corp.
    L.L. Thompson   - L.L. Thompson

20.____

4 (#2)

LIST 21   21.____
   92839102837   - 92839102837
   58891028   - 58891028
   7291728   - 7291928
   272839102839   - 272839102839
   428192   - 428102

LIST 22   22.____
   K.L. Veiller   - K.L. Veiller
   Webster, Roy   - Webster, Ray
   Drasner Spring Co.   - Drasner Spring Co.
   Edward J. Cravenport - Edward J. Cravanport
   Harold Field   - Harold A. Field

LIST 23   23.____
   2293   - 2293
   4283910293   - 5382910292
   871928374012   - 871928374912
   68293   - 68393
   8120364927   - 81293649271

LIST 24   24.____
   Tappe, Inc   - Tappe, Inc.
   A.M. Wentingworth   - A.M. Wentinworth
   Scott A. Elliott   - Scott A. Elliott
   Echeverria Corp.   - Echeverria Corp.
   Bradford Victor Company - Bradford Victer Company

LIST 25   25.____
   4820384   - 4820384
   393019283745   - 283919283745
   63917102   - 63927102
   91029354829   - 91029354829
   48291728   - 48291728

KEY (CORRECT ANSWERS)

1.	1	11.	1
2.	3	12.	3
3.	2	13.	4
4.	2	14.	2
5.	4	15.	1
6.	2	16.	3
7.	3	17.	2
8.	4	18.	1
9.	2	19.	1
10.	3	20.	2

21.	3
22.	2
23.	1
24.	2
25.	4

CODING

EXAMINATION SECTION

COMMENTARY

An ingenious question-type called coding, involving elements of alphabetizing, filing, name and number comparison, and evaluative judgment and application, has currently won wide acceptance in testing circles for measuring clerical aptitude and general ability, particularly on the senior (middle) grades (levels).

While the directions for this question usually vary in detail, the candidate is generally asked to consider groups of names, codes, and numbers, and then, according to a given plan, to arrange codes in alphabetic order; to arrange these in numerical sequence; to re-arrange columns of names and numbers in correct order; to espy errors in coding; to choose the correct coding arrangement in consonance with the given directions and examples, etc.

This question-type appear to have few parameters in respect to form, substance, or degree of difficulty.

Accordingly, acquaintance with, and practice in, the coding question is recommended for the serious candidate.

TEST 1

DIRECTIONS: Questions 1 through 8 are to be answered on the basis of the code table and the instructions given below.

Code Letter for Traffic Problem	B	H	Q	J	F	L	M	I
Code Number for Action Taken	1	2	3	4	5	6	7	8

Assume that each of the capital letters on the above chart is a radio code for a particular traffic problem and that the number immediately below each capital letter is the radio code for the correct action to be taken to deal with the problem. For instance, "1" is the action to be taken to deal with problem "B", "2" is the action to be taken to deal with problem "H", and so forth.

In each question, a series of code letters is given in Column 1. Column 2 gives four different arrangements of code numbers. You are to pick the answer (A, B, C, or D) in Column 2 that gives the code numbers that match the code letters in the same order.

SAMPLE QUESTION

Column 1
BHLFMQ

Column 2
A. 125678
B. 216573
C. 127653
D. 126573

According to the chart, the code numbers that correspond to these code letters are as follows: B – 1, M – 2, L – 6, F – 5, M – 7, Q – 3. Therefore, the right answer is 126573. This answer is D in Column 2.

115

2 (#1)

	Column 1	Column 2	
1.	BHQLMI	A. 123456 B. 123567 C. 123678 D. 125678	1.____
2.	HBJQLF	A. 214365 B. 213456 C. 213465 D. 214387	2.____
3.	QHMLFJ	A. 321654 B. 345678 C. 327645 D. 327654	3.____
4.	FLQJIM	A. 543287 B. 563487 C. 564378 D. 654378	4.____
5.	FBIHMJ	A. 518274 B. 152874 C. 528164 D. 517842	5.____
6.	MIHFQB	A. 872341 B. 782531 C. 782341 D. 783214	6.____
7.	JLFHQIM	A. 465237 B. 456387 C. 4652387 D. 4562387	7.____
8.	LBJQIFH	A. 614382 B. 6134852 C. 61437852 D. 61431852	8.____

KEY (CORRECT ANSWERS)

1. C
2. A
3. D
4. B
5. A
6. B
7. C
8. A

TEST 2

DIRECTIONS: Each question or incomplete statement is followed by several suggested answers or completions. Select the one that BEST answers the question or completes the statement. *PRINT THE LETTER OF THE CORRECT ANSWER IN THE SPACE AT THE RIGHT.*

Questions 1-5.

DIRECTIONS: Questions 1 through 5 are based on the following list showing the name and number of each of nine inmates.

1. Johnson   4. Thompson   7. Gordon
2. Smith   5. Frank   8. Porter
3. Edwards   6. Murray   9. Lopez

Each question consists of 3 sets of numbers and letters. Each set should consist of the numbers of three inmates and the first letter of each of their names. The letters should be in the same order as the numbers. In at least two of the three choices, there will be an error. On your answer sheet, mark only that choice in which the letters correspond with the numbers and are in the same order. If all three sets are wrong, mark choice D in your answer space.

<u>SAMPLE QUESTION</u>
A. 386 EPM
B. 542 FST
C. 474 LGT

Since 3 corresponds to E for Edwards, 8 corresponds to P for Porter, and 6 corresponds to M for Murray, choice A is correct and should be entered in your answer space. Choice B is wrong because letters T and S have been reversed. Choice C is wrong because the first number, which is 4, does NOT correspond with the first letter of choice C, which is L. It should have been T. If choice A were also wrong, then D would be the correct answer.

1. A. 382 EGS   B. 461 TMJ   C. 875 PLF   1._____

2. A. 549 FLT   B. 692 MJS   C. 758 GSP   2._____

3. A. 936 LEM   B. 253 FSE   C. 147 JTL   3._____

4. A. 569 PML   B. 716 GJP   C. 842 PTS   4._____

5. A. 356 FEM   B. 198 JPL   C. 637 MEG   5._____

Questions 6-10.

DIRECTIONS: Questions 6 through 10 are to be answered on the basis of the following information:

2 (#3)

In order to make sure stock is properly located, incoming units are stored as follows:

STOCK NUMBERS	BIN NUMBERS
00100 – 39999	D30, L44
40000 – 69999	14L, D38
70000 – 99999	41L, 80D
100000 and over	614, 83D

Using the above table, choose the answer A, B, C, or D, which lists the correct Bin Number for the Stock Number given.

6. 17243
   A. 41L   B. 83D   C. 14L   D. D30   6.____

7. 9219
   A. D38   B. L44   C. 614   D. 41L   7.____

8. 90125
   A. 41L   B. 614   C. D38   D. D30   8.____

9. 10001
   A. L44   B. D38   C. 80D   D. 83D   9.____

10. 200100
    A. 41L   B. 14L   C. 83D   D. D30   10.____

KEY (CORRECT ANSWERS)

1.	B	6.	D
2.	D	7.	B
3.	A	8.	A
4.	C	9.	A
5.	C	10.	C

TEST 3

DIRECTIONS: Each question or incomplete statement is followed by several suggested answers or completions. Select the one that BEST answers the question or completes the statement. *PRINT THE LETTER OF THE CORRECT ANSWER IN THE SPACE AT THE RIGHT.*

Questions 1-9.

DIRECTIONS: Assume that the Police Department is planning to conduct a statistical study of individuals who have been convicted of crimes during a certain year. For the purpose of this study, identification numbers are being assigned to individuals in the following manner:

The first two digits indicate the age of the individual.
The third digit indicates the sex of the individual:
    1. Male
    2. Female
The fourth digit indicates the type of crime involved:
    1. criminal homicide
    2. forcible rape
    3. robbery
    4. aggravated assault
    5. burglary
    6. larceny
    7. auto theft
    8. other
The fifth and sixth digits indicate the month in which the conviction occurred:
    01.   January
    02.   February, etc.

Questions 1 through 9 are to be answered SOLELY on the basis of the above information and the following list of individuals and identification numbers.

Abbott, Richard	271304	Morris, Chris	212705
Collins, Terry	352111	Owens, William	231412
Elders, Edward	191207	Parker, Leonard	291807
George, Linda	182809	Robinson, Charles	311102
Hill, Leslie	251702	Sands, Jean	202610
Jones, Jackie	301106	Smith, Michael	42108
Lewis, Edith	402406	Turner, Donald	191601
Mack, Helen	332509	White, Barbara	242803

1. The number of women on the above list is
   A. 6   B. 7   C. 8   D. 9

1._____

2. The two convictions which occurred during February were for the crimes of
    A. aggravated assault and auto theft
    B. auto theft and criminal homicide
    C. burglary and larceny
    D. forcible rape and robbery

3. The ONLY man convicted of auto theft was
    A. Richard Abbott   B. Leslie Hill
    C. Chris Morris   D. Leonard Parker

4. The number of people on the list who were 25 years old or older is
    A. 6   B. 7   C. 8   D. 9

5. The OLDEST person on the list is
    A. Terry Collins   B. Edith Lewis
    C. Helen Mack   D. Michael Smith

6. The two people on the list who are the same age are
    A. Richard Abbott and Michael Smith
    B. Edward Elders and Donald Turner
    C. Linda George and Helen Mack
    D. Leslie Hill and Charles Robinson

7. A 28-year-old man who was convicted of aggravated assault in October would have identification number
    A. 281410   B. 281509   C. 282311   D. 282409

8. A 33-year-old woman convicted in April of criminal homicide would have identification number
    A. 331140   B. 331204   C. 332014   D. 332104

9. The number of people on the above list who were convicted during the first six months of the year is
    A. 6   B. 7   C. 8   D. 9

Questions 10-19.

DIRECTIONS: The following is a list of patients who were referred by various clinics to the laboratory for tests. After each name is a patient identification number. Questions 10 through 19 are to be answered on the basis of the information contained in this list and the explanation accompanying it.

The first digit refers to the clinic which made the referral:
1. cardiac   6. Hematology
2. Renal   7. Gynecology
3. Pediatrics   8. Neurology
4. Ophthalmology   9. Gastroenterology
5. Orthopedics

The second digit refers to the sex of the patient:
1. male
2. female

The third and fourth digits give the age of the patient

The last two digits give the day of the month the laboratory tests were performed

LABORATORY REFERRALS DURING JANUARY

Adams, Jacqueline	320917	Miller, Michael	511806
Black, Leslie	813406	Pratt, William	214411
Cook, Marie	511616	Rogers, Ellen	722428
Fisher, Pat	914625	Saunders, Sally	310229
Jackson, Lee	923212	Wilson, Jan	416715
James, Linda	624621	Wyatt, Mark	321326
Lane, Arthur	115702		

10. According to the list, the number of women referred to the laboratory during January was
    A. 4 B. 5 C. 6 D. 7

11. The clinic from which the MOST patients were referred was
    A. Cardiac
    B. Gynecology
    C. Ophthalmology
    D. Pediatrics

12. The YOUNGEST patient referred from any clinic other than Pediatrics was
    A. Leslie Black
    B. Marie Cook
    C. Arthur Lane
    D. Sally Saunders

13. The number of patients whose laboratory tests were performed on or before January 16 was
    A. 7 B. 8 C. 9 D. 10

14. The number of patients referred for laboratory tests who are under age 45 is
    A. 7 B. 8 C. 9 D. 10

15. The OLDEST patient referred to the clinic during January was
    A. Jacqueline Adams
    B. Linda James
    C. Arthur Lane
    D. Jan Wilson

16. The ONLY patient treated in the Orthopedics clinic was
    A. Marie Cook
    B. Pat Fisher
    C. Ellen Rogers
    D. Jan Wilson

17. A woman, age 37 was referred from the Hematology clinic to the laboratory. Her laboratory tests were performed on January 9.
    Her identification number would be
    A. 610937 B. 623709 C. 613790 D. 623790

18. A man was referred for lab tests from the Orthopedics clinic. He is 30 years old and his tests were performed on January 6.
His identification number would be
A. 413006	B. 510360	C. 513006	D. 513060

18.____

19. A 4-year-old boy was referred from the Pediatrics clinic to have laboratory tests on January 23.
His identification number was
A. 310422	B. 310423	C. 310433	D. 320403

19.____

KEY (CORRECT ANSWERS)

1.	B	11.	D
2.	B	12.	B
3.	B	13.	A
4.	D	14.	C
5.	D	15.	D
6.	B	16.	A
7.	A	17.	B
8.	D	18.	C
9.	C	19.	B
10.	B		

TEST 4

DIRECTIONS: Each question or incomplete statement is followed by several suggested answers or completions. Select the one that BEST answers the question or completes the statement. *PRINT THE LETTER OF THE CORRECT ANSWER IN THE SPACE AT THE RIGHT.*

Questions 1-10.

DIRECTIONS: Questions 1 through 10 are to be answered on the basis of the information and directions given below.

Assume that you are a Senior Stenographer assigned to the personnel bureau of a city agency. Your supervisor has asked you to classify the employees in your agency into the following five groups:

- A. Employees who are college graduates, who are at least 35 years of age but less than 50, and who have been employed by the City for five years or more;
- B. Employees who have been employed by the City for less than five years, who are not college graduates, and who earn at least $32,500 a year but less than $34,500;
- C. Employees who have been City employees for five years or more, who are at least 21 years of age but less than 35, and who are not college graduates;
- D. Employee who earn at least $34,500 a year but less than $36,000 who are college graduates, and who have been employed by the City for less than five years;
- E. Employees who are not included in any of the foregoing groups.

NOTE: In classifying these employees you are to compute age and period of service as of January 1, 2003. In all cases, it is to be assumed that each employee has been employed continuously in City service. In each question, consider only the information which will assist you in classifying each employee Any information which is of no assistance in classifying an employee would not be considered.

SAMPLE: Mr. Brown, a 29-year-old veteran, was appointed to his present position of Clerk on June 1, 2000. He has completed two years of college. His present salary is $33,050.

The correct answer to this sample is B, since the employee has been employed by the City for less than five years, is not a college graduate, and earn at least $32,500 a year but less than $34,500.

Questions 1 through 10 contain excerpts from the personnel records of 10 employees in the agency. In the correspondingly numbered space at the right print the capital letter preceding the appropriate group into which you would place each employee.

1. Mr. James has been employed by the City since 1993, when he was graduated from a local college. Now 35 years of age, he earns $36,000 a year.   1.____

2. Mr. Worth began working in City service early in 1999. He was awarded his college degree in 1994, at the age of 21. As a result of a recent promotion, he now earns $34,500 a year.   2.____

2 (#4)

3. Miss Thomas has been a City employee since August 1, 1998. Her salary is $34,500 a year. Miss Thomas, who is 25 years old, has had only three years of high school training.

3.____

4. Mr. Williams has had three promotions since entering City service on January 1, 1991. He was graduated from college with honors in 1974, when he was 20 years of age. His present salary is $37,000 a year.

4.____

5. Miss Jones left college after two years of study to take an appointment to a position in the City service paying $33,300 a year. She began work on March 1, 1997 when she was 19 years of age.

5.____

6. Mr. Smith was graduated from an engineering college with honors in January 1998 and became a City employee three months later. His present salary is $35,810. Mr. Smith was born in 1976.

6.____

7. Miss Earnest was born on May 31, 1979. Her education consisted of four years of high school and one year of business school. She was appointed as a typist in a City agency on June 1, 1997. Her annual salary is $33,500.

7.____

8. Mr. Adams, a 24-year-old clerk, began his City service on July 1, 1999, soon after being discharged from the U.S. Army. A college graduate, his present annual salary is $33,200.

8.____

9. Miss Charles attends college in the evenings, hoping to obtain her degree is 2004, when she will be 30 years of age. She has been a City employee since April 1998, and earns $33,350.

9.____

10. Mr. Dolan was just promoted to his present position after six years of City service. He was graduated from high school in 1982, when he was 18 years of age, but did not go on to college. Mr. Dolan's present salary is $33,500.

10.____

KEY (CORRECT ANSWERS)

1.	A	6.	D
2.	D	7.	C
3.	E	8.	E
4.	A	9.	B
5.	C	10.	E

TEST 5

DIRECTIONS: Questions 1 through 4 each contain five numbers that should be arranged in numerical order. The number with the lowest numerical value should be first and the number with the highest numerical value should be last. Pick that option which indicates the CORRECT order of the numbers.

Examples: A. 9; 18; 14; 15; 27
                  B. 9; 14; 15; 18; 27
                  C. 14; 15; 18; 27; 9
                  D. 9; 14; 15; 27; 18

The correct answer is B, which contains the proper arrangement of the five numbers.

1.   A. 20573; 20753; 20738; 20837; 20098
    B. 20098; 20753; 20573; 20738; 20837
    C. 20098; 20573; 20753; 20837; 20738
    D. 20098; 20573; 20738; 20753; 20837

2.   A. 113492; 113429; 111314; 113114; 131413
    B. 111314; 113114; 113429; 113492; 131413
    C. 111314; 113429; 113492; 113114; 131413
    D. 111314; 113114; 131413; 113429; 113492

3.   A. 1029763; 1030421; 1035681; 1036928; 1067391
    B. 1030421; 1029763; 1035681; 1067391; 1036928
    C. 1030421; 1035681; 1036928; 1067391; 1029763
    D. 1029763; 1039421; 1035681; 1067391; 1036928

4.   A. 1112315; 1112326; 1112337; 1112349; 1112306
    B. 1112306; 1112315; 1112337; 1112326; 1112349
    C. 1112306; 1112315; 1112326; 1112337; 1112349
    D. 1112306; 1112326; 1112315; 1112337; 1112349

1.____
2.____
3.____
4.____

KEY (CORRECT ANSWERS)

1. D
2. B
3. A
4. C

TEST 6

DIRECTIONS: The phonetic filing system is a method of filing names in which the alphabet is reduced to key code letters. The six key letters and their equivalents are as follows:

KEY LETTERS	EQUIVALENTS
b	p, f, v
c	s, k, g, j, q, x, z
d	t
l	none
m	n
r	none

A key letter represents itself.
Vowels (a, e, i, o, and u) and the letters w, h, and y are omitted.
For example, the name GILMAN would be represented as follows:
  G is represented by the key letter C.
  I is a vowel and is omitted.
  L is a letter and represents itself.
  M is a key letter and represents itself.
  A is a vowel and is omitted.
  N is represented by the key letter M.

Therefore, the phonetic filing code for the name GILMAN is CLMM.

Answer Questions 1 through 10 based on the information below.

1. The phonetic filing code for the name FITZGERALD would be
   A. BDCCRLD   B. BDCRLD   C. BDZCRLD   D. BTZCRLD

2. The phonetic filing code CLBR may represent any one of the following names EXCEPT
   A. Calprey   B. Flower   C. Glover   D. Silver

3. The phonetic filing code LDM may represent any one of the following names EXCEPT
   A. Halden   B. Hilton   C. Walton   D. Wilson

4. The phonetic filing code for the name RODRIGUEZ would be
   A. RDRC   B. RDRCC   C. RDRCZ   D. RTRCC

5. The phonetic filing code for the name MAXWELL would be
   A. MCLL   B. MCWL   C. MCWLL   D. MXLL

6. The phonetic filing code for the name ANDERSON would be
   A. AMDRCM   B. ENDRSM   C. MDRCM   D. NDERCN

7. The phonetic filing code for the name SAVITSKY would be
   A. CBDCC   B. CBDCY   C. SBDCC   D. SVDCC

8. The phonetic filing code CMC may represent any one of the following names EXCEPT
   A. James B. Jayes C. Johns D. Jones

   8.____

9. The ONLY one of the following names that could be represented by the phonetic filing code CDDDM would be
   A. Catalano B. Chesterton C. Cittadino D. Cuttlerman

   9.____

10. The ONLY one of the following names that could be represented by the phonetic filing code LLMCM would be
    A. Ellington B. Hallerman C. Inslerman D. Willingham

    10.____

KEY (CORRECT ANSWERS)

1.	A	6.	C
2.	B	7.	A
3.	D	8.	B
4.	B	9.	C
5.	A	10.	D

COMMON DIAGNOSTIC NORMS

CONTENTS

		Page
1.	Respiration	1
2.	Pulse-Rate	1
3.	Blood Pressure	1
4.	Blood Metabolism	1
5.	Blood	1
6.	Urine	3
7.	Spinal Fluid	4
8.	Snellen Chart Fractions	4

COMMON DIAGNOSTIC NORMS

1. RESPIRATION: From 16-20 per minute.

2. PULSE-RATE: Men, about 72 per minute.
   Women, about 80 per minute.

3. BLOOD PRESSURE:
   Men: 110-135 (Systolic)   Women: 95-125   (Systolic)
        70-85   (Diastolic)   65-70   (Diastolic)

4. BASAL METABOLISM: Represents the body energy expended to maintain respiration, circulation, etc. Normal rate ranges from plus 10 to minus 10.

5. BLOOD:

   a. Red Blood (Erythrocyte) Count:
   Male adult - 5,000,000 per cu. mm.
   Female adult - 4,500,000 per cu. mm.
      (Increased in polycythemia vera, poisoning by carbon monoxide, in chronic pulmonary artery sclerosis, and in concentration of blood by sweating, vomiting, or diarrhea.)
      (Decreased in pernicious anemia, secondary anemia, and hypochronic anemia.)
   b. White Blood (Leukocyte) Count: 6,000 to 8,000 per cu. mm.
      (Increased with muscular exercise, acute infections, intestinal obstruction, coronary thrombosis, leukemias.)
      (Decreased due to injury to source of blood formation and interference in delivery of cells to bloodstream, typhoid, pernicious anemia, arsenic and benzol poisoning.)
      The total leukocyte group is made up of a number of diverse varieties of white blood cells. Not only the total leukocyte count, but also the relative count of the diverse varieties, is an important aid to diagnosis. In normal blood, from:
      70-72% of the leukocytes are *polymorphonuclear neuirophils.*
      2-4% of the leukocytes are *polymorphonuclear eosinophils.*
      0-.5% of the leukocytes are *basophils,*
      20-25% of the leukocytes are *lymphocytes.*
      2-6% of the leukocytes are *monocytes.*
   c. Blood Platelet (Thrombocyte) Count:
      250,000 per cu. mm. Blood platelets are important in blood coagulation.

   d. Hemoglobin Content:
      May normally vary from 85-100%. A 100% hemoglobin content is equivalent to the presence of 15.6 grams of hemoglobin in 100 c.c. of blood.
   e. Color Index:
      Represents the relative amount of hemoglobin contained in a red blood corpuscle compared with that of a normal individual of the patient's age and sex.
      The normal is 1. To determine the color index, the percentage of hemoglobin is divided by the ratio of red cells in the patient's blood to a norm of 5,000,000. Thus, a hemoglobin content of 60% and a red cell count of 4,000,000 (80% of 5,000,000) produces an abnormal color index of .75.

f. Sedimentation Rate:
   Represents the measurement of the speed with which red cells settle toward the bottom of a containing vessel. The rate is expressed in millimeters per hour, and indicates the total sedimentation of red blood cells at the end of 60 minutes.
   Average rate: 4-7 mm. in 1 hour
   Slightly abnormal rate: 8-15 mm. in 1 hour
   Moderately abnormal rate: 16-40 mm. in 1 hour
   Considerably abnormal rate: 41-80 mm. in 1 hour
   (The sedimentation rate is above normal in patients with chronic infections, or in whom there is a disease process involving destruction of tissue, such as coronary thrombosis, etc.)
g. Blood Sugar:
   90-120 mg. per 100 c.c. (Normal)
   In mild diabetics: 150-300 mg. per 100 c.c.
   In severe diabetics: 300-1200 mg. per 100 c.c.
h. Blood Lead:
   0.1 mg. or less in 100 c.c. (Normal). Greatly increased in lead poisoning.
i. Non-Protein Nitrogen:
   Since the function of the kidneys is to remove from the blood certain of the waste products of cellular activity, any degree of accumulation of these waste products in the blood is a measure of renal malfunction. For testing purposes, the substances chosen for measurement are the nitrogen-containing products of protein combustion, their amounts being estimated in terms of the nitrogen they contain. These substances are urea, uric acid, and creatinine, the sum total of which, in addition to any traces of other waste products, being designated as total non-protein nitrogen (NPN).

   The normal limits of NPN in 100 c.c. of blood range from 25-40 mg. Of this total, urea nitrogen normally constitutes 12-15 mg., uric acid 2-4 mg., and creatinine 1-2 mg.

6. URINE:

   a. Urine - Lead:
      0.08 mg. per liter of urine (normal).
      (Increased in lead poisoning.)
   b. Sugar:
      From none to a faint trace (normal).
      From 0.5% upwards (abnormal).
      (Increased in diabetes mellitus.)
   c. Urea:
      Normal excretion ranges from 15-40 grams in 24 hours.
      (Increased in fever and toxic states.)
   d. Uric Acid:
      Normal excretion is variable. (Increased in leukemia and gout.)
   e. Albumin:
      Normal renal cells allow a trace of albumin to pass into the urine, but this trace is so minute that it cannot be detected by ordinary tests.

f. Casts:
In some abnormal conditions, the kidney tubules become lined with substances which harden and form a mould or *oast* inside the tubes. These are later washed out by the urine, and may be detected microscopically. They are named either from the substance composing them, or from their appearance. Thus, there are pus casts, epithelial casts from the walls of the tubes, hyaline casts formed from coagulable elements of the blood, etc.

g. Pus Cells:
These are found in the urine in cases of nephritis or other inflammatory conditions of the urinary tract.

h. Epithelial Cells:
These are always present in the urine. Their number is greatly multiplied, however, in inflammatory conditions of the urinary tract.

i. Specific Gravity:
This is the ratio between the weight of a given volume of urine to that of the same volume of water. A normal reading ranges from 1.015 to 1.025. A high specific gravity usually occurs in diabetes mellitus. A low specific gravity is associated with a polyuria.

7. SPINAL FLUID:

a. Spinal Fluid Pressure (Manometric Reading):
100-200 mm. of water or 7-15 mm, of mercury (normal).
(Increased in cerebral edema, cerebral hemorrhage, meningitis, certain brain tumors, or if there is some process blocking the fluid circulation in the spinal column, such as a tumor or herniated nucleus pulposus impinging on the spinal canal.)

b. Quickenstedt's Sign:
When the veins in the neck are compressed on one or both sides, there is a rapid rise in the pressure of the cerebrospinal fluid of healthy persons, and this rise quickly disappears when pressure is removed from the neck. But when there is a block of the vertebral canal, the pressure of the cerebrospinal fluid is little or not at all affected by this maneuver.

c. Cerebrospinal Sugar:
50-60 mg. per 100 c.c. of spinal fluid (normal).
(Increased in epidemic encephalitis, diabetes mellitus, and increased intracranial pressure.)
(Decreased in purulent and tuberculous meningitis.)

d. Cerebrospinal Protein:
15-40 mg. per 100 c.c. of spinal fluid (normal).
(Increased in suppurative meningitis, epileptic seizures, cerebrospinal syphilis, anterior poliomyelitis, brain abscess, and brain tumor.)

e. Colloidal Gold Test:
This test is made to determine the presence of cerebrospinal protein.

f. Cerebrospinal Cell Count:
0-10 lymphocytes per cu. mm. (normal).

g. Cerebrospinal Globulin:
Normally negative. It is positive in various types of meningitis, various types of syphilis of the central nervous system, in poliomyelitis, in brain tumor, and in intracranial hemorrhage.

8. **SNELLEN CHART FRACTIONS AS SCHEDULE LOSS DETERMINANTS:**

   a. Visual acuity is expressed by a Snell Fraction, where the numerator represents the distance, in feet, between the subject and the test chart, and the denominator represents the distance, in feet, at which a normal eye could read a type size which the abnormal eye can read only at 20 feet.
   b. Thus, 20/20 means that an individual placed 20 feet from the test chart clearly sees the size of type that one with normal vision should see at that distance.
   c. 20/60 means that an individual placed 20 feet from the test chart can read only a type size, at a distance of 20 feet, which one of normal vision could read at 60 feet.
   d. Reduction of a Snellen Fraction to its simplest form roughly indicates the amount of vision remaining in an eye. Thus, a visual acuity of 20/60 corrected implies a useful vision of 1/3 or 33 1/3%, and a visual loss of 2/3 or 66 2/3% of the eye.

   Similarly:

Visual Acuity (Corrected)	Percentage Loss of Use of Eye
20/20	No loss
20/25	20%
20/30	33 1/3%
20/40	50%
20/50	60%
20/60	66 2/3%
20/70	70% (app.)
20/80	75%
20/100	100% (since loss of 80% or more constitutes industrial blindness)

BASIC NURSING INFORMATION

I. COMMONLY USED ABBREVIATIONS

A

A	admission
A_2	aortic 2nd sound
AB	abortion
ABD	abdominal
ABE	acute bacterial endocarditis
ABG	arterial blood gases
abbr	abbreviations
ABS	abscess
ACDU	active duty
ACTH	adrenocorticotropic hormone
AD	right ear
ad lib	as desired
AFB	acid-fast bacillus
A/G	albumin-globulin ratio
Ag	silver
AJ	ankle jerk
AK	above knee
AKA	above knee amputation
ALB	albumin
ALK	alkaline
AM	morning
AMA	against medical advice American Medical Association
AMB	ambulatory
AM J NURS	American Journal of Nursing
amp	ampere
AMP	amputation
ANES	anesthesia
ANT	anterior
AOD	administrative officer of the day
AOW	admitted from other ward
A&P	anterior and posterior auscultation and percussion
As	arsenic
AS	left ear
ASAP	as soon as possible
ASCVD	arteriosclerotic/atherosclerotic cardiovascular disease
ASD	atrial septal defect
ASHD	arteriosclerotic heart disease
ASOT	antistreptolysin 0 titer
ATN	acute tubular necrosis
Au	gold
AUR FIB	auricular fibrillation
AU	both ears
AV	arteriovenous
AWOL	absent without leave
AZT	Aschheim-Zondek test

B

Ba	barium
BC	bone conduction
BCP	birth control pill
BE	barium enema
BID	twice a day
BIL	bilirubin
BJ	biceps jerk
BK	below knee
BKA	below knee amputation
BM	bowel movement
BMR	basal metabolism rate
BP	blood pressure
BPH	benign prostatic hypertrophy
BR	bed rest
BRP	bathroom privileges
BRc̄BRP	bed rest with bathroom privileges
BS	blood sugar
BSP	bromsulphalein
BTB	breakthrough bleeding
BTL	bilateral tubal ligation
BUN	blood urea nitrogen
B&W	black and white
BX	biopsy

C

c	with
C	carbon
	Celsius (centigrade)
	curie
$C_{1, 2, or 3}$	cervical 1, 2, or 3
Ca	cancer
	carcinoma
CAL	calorie
CAP	capacity
	capsule
CATH	catheter
CAUC	Caucasian
CBC	complete blood count
cc	cubic centimeter
CC	chief complaint
CCU	coronary care unit
CF	cystic fibrosis
CHF	congestive heart failure
CHO	carbohydrate
CHOL	cholesterol
Cl	chloride
CL	convalescent leave
CLR	census last report
cm	centimeter
CMAA	chief master-at-arms
cmm	cubic millimeter
CNS	central nervous system
Co	cobalt
CO	carbon monoxide compound
CO_2	carbon dioxide
C/O	complains of
cont	continue
	continuously
COPD	chronic obstructive pulmonary disease
CPD	cephalopelvic disproportion
CPK	creatinine phosphakinase
cps	cycles per second
CRP	C-reactive protein
CS	cervical spine
	cesarean section
C&S	culture and sensitivity
CSF	cerebrospinal fluid
CSS	central sterile supply
CV	cardiovascular
	central venous
CVA	cardiovascular/ cerebrovascular accident
CVD	cardiovascular disease
CVP	central venous pressure
CVRD	cardiovascular renal disease
CX	cervix

D

db	decibel
DC	direct current
	discharge
	discontinue
D&C	dilatation and curettage
DD	discharged by death
DEC	deceased
DEP	dependent
DEP/D	dependent daughter
DEP/F	dependent father
DEP/M	dependent mother
DEP/MIL	dependent mother-in-law
DEP/S	dependent son
DEP/W	dependent wife
DEPT	department
DERM	dermatology
DF	dorsiflexion
DIFF	differential
DISCH	discharge
DISP	disposition
	dispensary
DM	diabetes mellitus
DOA	dead on arrival
DOB	date of birth
DOD	day of delivery
DOE	dyspnea on exertion
DOS	day of surgery

DP	dorsalis pedis	DU	diagnosis undetermined
DPT	dyptheria, pertussis, and tetanus	D/W	dextrose in water
dr	dram	DX	diagnosis
DR	doctor	D5NS	5% dextrose in normal saline
DT	delirium tremens	D5W	5% dextrose in water
DTK	deep tendon reflex		

E

ea	each	EPIS	episiotomy
EBL	estimated blood loss	EPITH	epithelial
EC	enteric-coated	ER	emergency room
ECG	electrocardiogram	ESR	erythrocyte sedimentation
ECT	electroconvulsive therapy	EST	electroshock therapy
EDC	estimated date of confinement	ET	endotracheal
		ETH	elixir terpin hydrate
EEG	electroencephalogram	ETH/C	elixir terpin hydrate with codeine
EENT	eye, ear, nose, and throat	ETOH	ethyl alcohol
EIP	extensor indicis proprius	EXAM	examination
		exp	expended
ELFD	elective low forceps delivery	ext	extended extension
ELIX	elixir	EXT	extraction external extremity
ENT	ear, nose, and throat		
EOM	extraocular movement		
EOS	eosinophils		

F

F	Fahrenheit	fl oz	fluid ounce
FB	foreign body	FORMIL	foreign military
FBS	fasting blood sugar	FR	French, catheter (use only with a number)
F/C	fracture, compound		
F/C/C	fracture, compound, comminuted	F/S	fracture, simple
		F/S/C	fracture, simple, comminuted
Fe	iron	ft	foot feet
FFP	fresh frozen plasma		
FEM	female	FUO	fever of undetermined origin
FH	family history fetal head fetal heart	FX	fracture
		FY	fiscal year
FHR	fetal heart rate		
FHS	fetal heart sounds		
FHT	fetal heart tones		

G

g	gram
ga	gauge
GA	gastric analysis
GB	gallbladder
GC	gonococcus
GI	gastrointestinal
gr	grain
GRAV i	primigravida
GSR	galvanic skin response
GSW	gunshot wound
gtt	drop
GTT	glucose tolerance test
GU	genitourinary
GV	gentian violet
GYN	gynecology

H

H	hydrogen
HA	headache
HCG	human chorionic gonadotropin
HC1	hydrochloric acid
HCT	hematocrit
HCVD	hypertensive cardiovascular disease
HD	hearing distance
HEENT	head, eyes, ear, nose, and throat
Hg	mercury
HG	hemoglobin
HNP	herniated nucleus pulposus
HOSP	hospital
HPI	history of present illness
hr	hour
HR	Health Record
HS	(hora somni) on retiring
HSS	hot saline soaks
ht	height
HX	history
HC1	hydrochloride

I

I	iodine
IBC	iron-binding capacity
IC	intercostal, intracranial
ICP	intracranial pressure
ICS	intercostal space
ICU	intensive care unit
ID	identification
I&D	incision and drainage
IM	intramuscular
IMP	impression
in	inch
INHAL	inhalation
INJ	inject
INSTR	instruction
I&O	intake and output
IP	interphalangeal

J

JAMA	Journal of the American Medical Association
JCAH	Joint Commission on Accreditation of Hospitals

K

K	potassium
KCl	potassium chloride
kg	kilogram
KI	potassium iodide
KJ	knee jerk
KLS	kidney, liver, spleen
KUB	kidney, ureters, bladder
KVO	keep vein open

L

l	liter
L	left
L&A	light and accommodation
LAB	laboratory
LAT	lateral
lb	pound
LBBB	left bundle branch block
LBP	lower back pain
LCCA	left common carotid artery
LDH	lactic dehydrogenase
LE	lupus erythematosus
LFT	liver function test
lg	large
LGA	large for gestational age
LIB	liberty
LIQ	liquid
LLE	left lower extremity
LLL	left lower lobe
LLQ	left lower quadrant
LMP	last menstrual period
LNMP	last normal menstrual period
LOA	left occipitoanterior
LOC	level of consciousness
LoNa	low sodium
LOP	left occipitoposterior
LP	lumbar puncture
LPN	licensed practical nurse
LUL	left upper lobe
LUQ	left upper quadrant

M

m	meter minim (equivalent to a drop)
MI	mitral first heart sound
MAA	master at arms
HAND	mandible
MAR	Medication Administration Record
MAX	maxilla maximum
mc	millicurie
MED	medical medicine
meq	milliequivalent
mg	milligram
mg/100 ml	milligrams per 100 ml
Mg	magnesium
MI	myocardial infarction
min	minute minim
MIP	middle interphalangeal
ml	milliliter
mm	millimeter
MO	medical officer
MOD	medical officer of the day
MS	multiple sclerosis

N

N	nitrogen
Na	sodium
NA	nurse's assistant
NaCl	sodium chloride (salt)
NB	newborn
NCD	not considered disqualifying
nec	not elsewhere classified
NEC	negative
NEURO	neurology
NF	National Formulary
NG	nasogastric
NIS	not in stock
NNP	no nocturnal paroxysms
No	number
NOC	nocturnal
NP	neuropsychiatric
NPH	neutral protamine hegedorn
NPN	nonprotein nitrogen
NPO	nothing by mouth
NS	normal saline
NSR	normal sinus rhythm
NSS	normal saline solution
NSU	nonspecific urethritis
NT	nasotracheal
NTG	nontoxic goiter
N&V	nausea and vomiting
NWB	no weight bearing

O

O	oral
O_2	oxygen
OB	obstetrics
OBST	obstruction
OCC	occupied / occult / occasional
OCT	Oxytocin Challenge Test
OD	right eye
oint	ointment
OP	operation
O&P	ova and parasites
OPD	outpatient department
OPS	outpatient service
OR	operating room
ORTHO	orthopedics
OS	left eye
OT	occupational therapy
OU	both eyes
oz	ounce

P

P	phosphorus pulse
P₂	pulmonic second sound
PA	physician's assistant
PA&LAT	posterioanterior and lateral
P&A	percussion and auscultation
PAL	prisoner at large
PAP	papanicolaou (smear)
PAT	paroxysmal atrial tachycardia
per	through by means of
PERLA	pupils equal, and react to light and accommodation
pH	hydrogen ion concentration
PH	past history personal history public health
PHAR	pharmacy
PI	present illness
PID	pelvic inflammatory disease
PIP	proximal interphalan- geal
PKU	phenylketonuria
PM	afternoon evening postmortem
PO	by mouth phone order postoperative
POD	postoperative day
POV	privately owned vehicle
PP	postpartum after delivery postprandial
PPBS	postprandial blood sugar
PBI	protein-bound iodine
PC	after meals
pCO_2	carbon dioxide pressure
PCV	packed cell volume
PDA	patent ductus arteriosus
PDR	Physician's Desk Reference
PE	physical examination
PEDS	pediatrics
PEG	pneumoencephalogram
PPD	purified protein derivative
PPM	parts per million
pr	pair
PR	pulse rate
PRE	passive resistance exercises
PREG	pregnant
PREOP	preoperative
PREP	prepare
PRN	(pro re nata) when necessary
PRO	prothrombin
PROCTO	proctosigmoidoscopy
PROM	premature rupture of membrane
PSP	phenolsulfonphthalein
pt	pint
PT	prothrombin time physical therapy
PTA	prior to admission
PTB	patella tendon bearing
PTT	partial thromboplastin test
PUD	pregnancy, uterine, delivered
PUND	pregnancy, uterine, not delivered
PVC	premature ventricular contraction

Q

Q	every
QAM	every morning
QD	every day
QH	every hour
Q2H	every 2 hours
Q3H	every 3 hours
Q4H	every 4 hours
Q6H	every 6 hours
Q8H	every 8 hours
QID	four times a day
QNS	quantity not sufficient
QOD	every other day
QPM	every evening
QS	quantity sufficient (sufficient quantity)
qt	quart
QUAL	quality qualitative
QUANT	quantity quantitative

R

R	right rectal respiration
Ra	radium
RAI	radioactive iodine
RAIU	radioactive iodine uptake
RBBB	right bundle branch block
RBC	red blood cell red blood count
RCCA	right common carotid artery
RDS	respiratory distress syndrome
REHAB	rehabilitation
REL	religion
REM	rapid eye movement
RESP	respirator respiratory
RF	rheumatic fever
Rh	Rhesus factor
RHD	rheumatic heart disease
RL	Ringer's lactate
RLL	right lower lobe
RLQ	right lower quadrant
R&M	routine and microscopic
RML	right middle lobe
RN	registered nurse
ROA	right occipitoanterior
ROM	range of motion
ROP	right occipitoposterior
ROS	review of systems
RR&E	round, regular, and equal
RSR	regular sinus rhythm
RUL	right upper lobe
RUQ	right upper quadrant
RX	take treatment

S

S	without
S	sulfur
SA	sinoatrial
S&A	sugar and acetone
SAH	subsist at home
SC	subcutaneous
SF	standard form
SG	specific gravity
SGA	small for gestational age
SGD	straight gravity drainage
SCOT	serum glutamic-oxaloacetic transaminase
SH	social history
SIG	let it be marked
SI joint	sacro iliac joint
SIQ	sick in quarters
SL	serious list
SLR	straight leg raising
SOB	short of breath
SOL	solution
SOP	standard operating procedure
SOQ	sick officer quarters
SOS	(si opus sit) if it is necessary
SP	specimen / spirit
SP GR	specific gravity
SR	sedimentation rate
SROM	spontaneous rupture of membranes
ss	one-half
S/S	signs and symptoms
SSE	soap suds enema
STAPH	staphalococcus
STAT	immediately
STREP	streptococcus
STS	serological test for syphilis
STSG	split thickness skin graft
SURG	surgical
SUSP	suspension
SVC	superior vena cava
SX	signs / symptoms
SYR	syrup

T

T	temperature
T&A	tonsillectomy and adenoidectomy
TAB	tablet
TAH	total abdominal hysterectomy
TBC	tuberculosis
tbsp	tablespoonful
TC	throat culture
TF	to follow
THER	therapy
TID	three times a day
TINCT	tincture
TM	tympanic membrane
TNTC	too numerous to count
TO	telephone order
TOW	transfer to other ward
TP	total protein
TPR	temperature, pulse, and respiration
TRMCA	thrombosis, right middle cerebral artery
tsp	teaspoonful
TT	thymol turbidity
TUR	transurethral resection
TVH	total vaginal hysterectomy
T&X-match	type and crossmatch

U

U	unit
UA	unauthorized leave
UCD	usual childhood diseases
UGI	upper gastrointestinal
UNG	ointment
U/0	urine output
UPJ	ureteropelvic junction
URI	upper respiratory infection
UTI	urinary tract infection
UVJ	ureterovesical junction
UVL	ultraviolet light

V

VA	Veterans Administration
VAB	Veterans Administration beneficiary
VAC	vacant beds
VAG	vagina, vaginal
VC	vital capacity
VD	venereal disease
VDRL	Venereal Disease Research Laboratories
VMA	vanil mandelic acid (vanillymandelic a.)
VO	verbal order
VS	vital signs
VSD	ventricular septal defect
VSL	very serious list

W

WBC	white blood cell
WD	ward, well-developed
WDWN	well-developed, well-nourished
WNL	within normal limits
WO	without
wt	weight
W/V	weight per volume

X

X	except
X	multiplied by

Y

YO	year old
YOB	year of birth

Z

Zn	zinc

II. SYMBOLS

Symbol	Meaning	Symbol	Meaning
Ⓛ	left	↑	elevation increased up
Ⓡ	right		
♂	male	°	degree
♀	female	'	foot
p̄	after	"	inch
#	gauge number weight	⋅⋅⁄′′	two
24°	24 hours	–	absent negative
ā	before	Rx	take
c̄	with	2°	secondary
s̄	without	2x x2	twice
?	question of questionable possible	1x x1	once
↓	decreased depression	>	greater than
		<	less than

145

III. CONVERSIONS OF DOSAGES

MILLIGRAMS (mg)	= GRAINS (gr)
1296	20
1000	15
300	5
100	1.5
60	1
50	3/4
30	1/2
20	1/4
15	1/6
10	
9	
8	
7	
6	
5	
4	
3	
2	1/30
1	1/60
0.9	
0.8	
0.7	
0.6	1/100
0.5	1/120
0.4	1/150
0.3	1/200
0.2	1/300
0.1	1/600
0.0	

MILLILITERS (ml)	= FLUID OUNCES (fl oz)
1000	32 (= 1 qt)
946.4	16 (= 1 pt)
473.2	
200	
120	4 (= 1/2 cup)
100	
90	
80	
70	
60	
50	
40	
30	
20	
15	1/2 (=1 tbsp)
10	
5	1/6 (= 1 tsp)
4	60 minims (1 fl dram)
3	
2	
1	
0	

IV. METRIC CONVERSION FACTORS
A. Approximate Conversions to Metric Measure

SYMBOL	WHEN YOU KNOW	MULTIPLY BY	TO FIND	SYMBOL
		LENGTH		
in	inches	2.5	centimeters	cm
ft	feet	30	centimeters	cm
yd	yards	0.9	meters	in
mi	miles	1.6	kilometers	km
		MASS (weight)		
oz	ounces	28	grams	g
lb	pounds	0.45	kilograms	kg
		VOLUME		
tsp	teaspoons	5	milliliters	ml
tbsp	tablespoons	15	milliliters	ml
fl oz	fluid ounces	30	milliliters	ml
c	cups	0.24	liters	l
pt	pints	0.47	liters	l
qt	quarts	0.95	liters	l
gal	gallons	3.8	liters	l
		TEMPERATURE (exact)		
°F	Fahrenheit	5/9 (after subtracting 32)	Celsius	°C

To convert a Fahrenheit reading to Celsius, subtract 32 from the Fahrenheit reading, multiply by 5, and divide by 9.

B. APPROXIMATE CONVERSIONS FROM METRIC MEASURES

SYMBOL	WHEN YOU KNOW	MULTIPLY BY	TO FIND	SYMBOL
		LENGTH		
mm	millimeters	0.04	inches	in
cm	centimeters	0.4	inches	in
m	meters	3.3	feet	ft
m	meters	1.1	yards	yd
		MASS (weight)		
g	grams	0.035	ounces	oz
kg	kilograms	2.2	pounds	1b
		VOLUME		
ml	milliliters	0.03	fluid ounces	fl oz
1	liters	2.1	pints	pt
1	liters	1.06	quarts	qt
1	liters	0.26	gallons	gal
		TEMPERATURE (exact)		
°C	Celsius	9/5 (then add 32)	Fahrenheit	°F

To convert a Celsius reading to Fahrenheit, divide degrees Celsius by 5, multiply by 9, and add 32.

CELSIUS (°C)	= FAHRENHEIT (°F)		CELSIUS (°C)	= FAHRENHEIT (°F)	
100.0	Water boils	212.0	36.9		
42.0		107.6	36.8		
41.0		105.8	36.7		98.0
40.3		104.2	36.6		
40.2		104.1	36.5		
40.0		104.0	36.4		
39.0		102.2	36.3		
38.9		102.0	36.2		
38.3		101.0	36.1		97.0
38.0		100.4	36.0		96.8
37.8		100.0	35.5		96.0
37.2		99.0	35.0		95.0
37.0	Normal body	98.6	34.0		94.0
			0.0	Water freezes	32.0

GLOSSARY OF MEDICAL TERMS (EYE, EAR, NOSE AND THROAT)

CONTENTS

	PAGE
ABDUCT ...... AUDIOMETER	1
AUDITORY CORTEX ...... COMPLAINT	2
COMPRESSION ...... EPITHELIUM	3
EQUILIBRIUM ...... FURUNCLE	4
GUSTATORY ...... INTRINSIC	5
LACERATION ...... MILLIMETER	6
MOLECULAR ...... OSTEOMYELITIS	7
OTOLARYNGOLOGIST ...... PSYCHIATRIC	8
PULMONARY ...... SPECULUM	9
SPHINCTER ...... TRAUMA	10
TRISMUS ...... VOCALIZATION	11

GLOSSARY OF MEDICAL TERMS (EYE, EAR, NOSE AND THROAT)

A

ABDUCT
To draw away from the median line. When the vocal cords abduct, they separate.
ACCELERATION
A quickening or speeding up.
ACOUSTIC
As pertaining to sound or to the sense of hearing.
ACUTE
Having a short and relatively severe course.
ADDUCT
To move towards the median. When the vocal cords adduct, they come together.
ADENOIDITIS
Inflammation of the adenoid tissue in the nasopharynx.
ALLERGEN
The material responsible for an allergic reaction.
AMPLIFY
The process of making larger or louder, as the increase of an auditory stimulus.
ANATOMY
The science of the structure of the body and the relation of its parts.
ANGINA
A severe pain.
ANGULAR
Sharply bent; having corners or angles.
ANTIBIOTIC
A chemical substance which has the capacity to inhibit the growth of or destroy bacteria and other microorganisms.
ANTIHISTAMINE
Any of several drugs used to minimize an allergic reaction.
ANTISEPTIC
A substance that will inhibit the growth and development of microorganisms.
ASCENT
A rising up. The amount of upward slope or elevation.
ASEPTIC
Not septic. Free from infectious material.
ASPIRATION
The removal of fluids or debris from a cavity by means of an aspirator.
ASTHMA
A disease marked by recurrent attacks of difficult breathing.
ATMOSPHERIC PRESSURE
The pressure due to the weight of the earth's atmosphere, equal at sea level to about 14.7 pounds per square inch.
AUDIOMETER
Device for testing the power of hearing.

AUDITORY CORTEX
  The sensory area of hearing located in the temporal lobe of the brain.
AURICLE
  That portion of the external ear not contained within the head.
AUTOCLAVE
  An apparatus for effecting sterilization by steam under pressure.

B

BACTERIA
  A loosely used generic name for any microorganism of the order Eubacteriales.
BACTERIAL
  Pertaining to or caused by bacteria.
BAROTRAUMA
  Injury caused by pressure, such as injury to the middle ear or sinus cavity due to difference in pressure between the atmosphere and the inside of the cavity.
BENIGN
  Not malignant.
BIFID
  Clefts into two parts or branches.
BILATERAL
  Having two sides or pertaining to two layers.

C

CANNULATION
  The insertion of a cannula into a hollow organ or body cavity.
CAUTERIZE
  To burn with a hot instrument or with a caustic substance so as to destroy tissue or prevent the spread of infection.
CELLULITIS
  Infection or inflammation of the loose subcutaneous tissue.
CENTIMETER
  A unit of measurement in the metric system. Being equal to 0.3937 inch.
CEREBRAL SPINAL FLUID
  A clear fluid contained within the cavities of and surrounding the brain and spinal cord.
CERUMEN
  The wax-like secretion found within the external auditory canal.
CHONDROMA
  A benign tumor of cartilage.
CHRONIC
  Persisting over a long period of time.
COMMINUTION
  Broken into small fragments.
COMPLAINT
  The symptom or group of symptoms about which the patient consults the physician.

COMPRESSION
  The act of pressing together to diminish volume and increase density.
CONCOMITANT
  Accompanying or joined with another.
CONGENITAL
  Existing at or before birth.
CULTURE
  The propagation of microorganisms in a special media.
CURRETAGE
  To remove by scraping.
CYCLES PER SECOND
  In audiology, the number of sound waves passing a point per second.
CYST
  A sac which contains a liquid or semisolid material.

D

DECAY
  The process of stage of decline. The decomposition of dead organic matter.
DECONGESTANT
  A drug which reduces congestion or swelling.
DEMARKATION
  Any dividing line apparent on the surface of the body, such as the boundary between normal and infected tissue.
DERMATITIS
  Inflammation of the skin.
DESCENT
  A coming down, going down, or downward motion.
DIPLOPIA
  Double vision.
DISCRIMINATION
  The ability to make or to perceive distinctions.

E

EDEMA
  The presence of abnormally large amounts of fluid in the intercellular tissue spaces of the body.
ENDOLYMPH
  The fluid contained in the membranous labyrinth of the ear.
ENOPHTHALMUS
  Abnormal retraction of the eye into the orbit.
ENTITY
  An independently existing thing; a reality.
EPISTAXIS
  Nose bleed or hemorrhage from the nose.
EPITHELIUM
  The covering of the internal and external surfaces of the body.

EQUILIBRIUM
A state of balance. A condition in which opposing forces exactly counteract each other.

ERYTHEMA
A name applied to redness of the skin produced by congestion of the capillaries. This may result in a variety of causes such as infection and trauma.

EUSTACHIAN TUBE
A slender tube between the middle ear and the pharynx which serves to equalize air pressure on both sides of the ear drum. Named after Bartolommeo Eustachio, an Italian anatomist.

EVACUATE
To make empty; to remove the contents.

EXACERBATION
An increase or recurrence in the severity of any symptom or disease.

EXCISION
An act of removing by cutting away.

EXOSTOSIS
An abnormal bony protuberance.

EXTRINSIC
Coming from or originating outside the organ or limb where found.

EXUDATE
Material such as fluid, cells, or cellular debris which has been deposited in or on tissue surfaces. This usually is the result of inflammation.

F

FIBROUS
Composed of or containing fibers.

FILAMENTOUS
Long, thread-like structures.

FIXATION
The act of holding, suturing, or fastening in a fixed position. Direction of a gaze so that the image of the object looked at falls on the fovea centralis.

FORAMEN
A natural opening or passage, especially a passage into or through a bone.

FREQUENCY
The number of vibrations made by a particle or ray per unit of time.

FUNCTIONAL HEARING LOSS
Hearing loss without an organic basis, such as malingering or psychological.

FUNGUS
A class of vegetable organisms of a low order of development which includes molds, mushrooms, and toadstools.

FURUNCLE
A painful nodule formed in the skin by bacteria which enter into the hair follicles causing a localized infection.

G

GUSTATORY
Pertaining to the sense of taste.

H

HEMATOMA
A swelling containing blood.
HERTZ
The international unit of frequency, equal to one cycle per second.
HIVES
An allergic skin condition characterized by itching, burning, and stinging during the formation of a red papular rash.
HYPERACTIVE
Abnormally increased activity.
HYPEREMIA
Redness of a part due to engorgement of blood vessels.
HYPERTENSION
Abnormally high blood pressure.
HYPERTROPHIC
The enlargement or overgrowth of an organ due to an increase in size of its cells.
HYPERVENTILATION
Abnormally rapid and deep breathing.
HYPOACTIVE
Abnormally diminished activity.
HYSTERIA
A psychoneurosis characterized by lack of control of emotions.

I

IMPREGNATE
To saturate one material with another, such as to saturate gauze with an ointment.
INBIBITION
The absorption of a liquid.
INCISION
A cut or a wound produced by cutting.
INFECTION
Invasion of the body by pathogenic microorganisms and the reaction of the tissue to their presence and to the toxins generated by the microorganisms.
INFLAMMATION
The condition into which tissues enter as a reaction to injury or infection. It is characterized by pain, heat, redness, and swelling of the area.
INTRINSIC
Situated entirely within or pertaining exclusively to a part.

L

LACERATION
A wound made by tearing.

LARYNGITIS
Inflammation of the larynx.

LARYNGOPHARYNX
That portion of the pharynx lying between the upper edge of the epiglottis and the vocal cords.

LATENT
Concealed or not yet manifest.

LATERAL
The position of a part further from midline than another part of the same side.

LESION
A pathologic or traumatic lack of continuity of tissue or loss of function of a part.

LEUKEMIA
A fatal disease of the blood-forming organs characterized by a marked increase in the number of white blood cells.

LINEAR
Pertaining to or resembling a line. Linear acceleration means acceleration in a straight line.

M

MALAISE
A vague feeling of discomfort.

MALIGNANT
As applied to tumors, malignant means the tendency to invade surrounding structures and the ability to spread to other parts of the body by way of the bloodstream or lymphatic channels.

MALINGERING
The faking or exaggeration of symptoms of an illness or injury.

MALOCCLUSION
The lack of occlusion between the maxillary and mandibular teeth which interferes with mastication.

MANIFEST
Something which is readily evident or clear to the sight or mind.

MARSUPIALIZATION
An operation which removes a portion of a cyst, abscess, or tumor, empties its contents, and sutures its edges to the line of incision.

MASTICATION
The chewing of food.

MEMBRANE
A layer of tissue which covers the surface or divides a space or organ.

MENINGITIS
An inflammation or infection of the meningeal covering of the brain.

MICRON
A unit of measurement equal to 1/1000th of a millimeter.

MILLIMETER
A unit of measurement equaling 1/1000th of a meter or 0.03937 inch.

MOLECULAR
   Pertaining to molecules or a chemical combination of two or more atoms.
MORBIDITY
   The condition of being diseased or sick.
MORTALITY
   Death.
MUCOSA
   The mucous membrane covering a surface such as the membrane covering the surface of the palate or tongue.
MYRINGITIS
   Inflammation of the tympanic membrane.
MYRINGOTOMY
   An incision through the tympanic membrane.
MYRINGOPLASTY
   The surgical repair of a perforation in the tympanic membrane.

N

NECROSIS
   The death of a tissue or a part.
NEOPLASM
   Any new growth or tumor. It may be either a benign or malignant process.
NYSTAGMUS
   An involuntary rapid movement of the eyeball which may be horizontal, vertical, or rotary.

O

OBJECTIVE
   Pertaining to things which are perceptible to the senses.
OCCLUSION
   The relationship of the maxillary and mandibular teeth when in functional contact.
OINTMENT
   A semisolid preparation for external application to the body.
OLFACTION
   The sense of smell or the act of smelling.
OMINOUS
   Serving as an omen, or having a character of an evil omen.
OPEN REDUCTION
   Reduction of a fracture after exposing the fracture by an incision.
ORGANISM
   A body of living material. It may be a single cell, plant, or animal.
ORIFICE
   The entrance or outlet of any body cavity.
OSSEOUS
   Bone or bony.
OSTEOMYELITIS
   Inflammation or infection of bone.

OTOLARYNGOLOGIST
A physician who has specialized in the surgical and medical treatment of diseases of the ear, nose, and throat.

OTORRHEA
A discharge from the ear.

OTOTOXIC
Pertaining to something which is toxic to the ear. Specifically, certain drugs destroy the minute sensory cells of the inner ear.

P

PARENTERAL
Refers to medicine given by the subcutaneous, intramuscular, or intravenous route.

PARESIS
Slight or incomplete paralysis.

PATENT
Open, unobstructed.

PATHOGENIC
Refers to an organism or substance capable of causing disease.

PEDIATRIC
That branch of medicine which treats children.

PERCEPTION
The awareness of objects or other data through the medium of the senses.

PERFORATE
To pierce with holes.

PERIPHERY
Away from center. Example: The finger is peripheral to the elbow.

PETROUS
Resembling a rock. The petrous bone is so-called because of its hardness.

PHARYNGITIS
Inflammation of the pharynx.

PHARYNX
The tube between the posterior portion of the mouth and nose above, and the trachea and esophagus below.

PRACTITIONER
An authorized practitioner of medicine.

PHYSIOLOGY
The science or study of the function of living organisms.

PITCH
The quality of sound dependent upon the frequency of vibration.

PNEUMATIZATION
The formation of air-filled cells or cavities in tissues. Especially such formation in the temporal bone.

PROPAGATE
To reproduce, multiply, or spread.

PROPHYLACTIC
An agent that tends to ward off disease.

PSYCHIATRIC
That branch of medicine which deals with disorders of the human mind.

PULMONARY
  Pertaining to the lungs.
PURULENT
  Consists of or contains pus.

Q

QUALITATIVE
  Having to do with the quality of something.
QUANTITATIVE
  Having to do with the quantity of something, capable of being measured.

R

RAPPORT
  A close or sympathetic relationship.
RAREFACTION
  The condition of being or becoming less dense.
REVOLUTION
  A turning or spinning motion of a body or thing around a center axis.
RHINORRHEA
  The discharge of material from the nose.
RHINOSCOPY
  The examination of the nasal passages.
ROENTGENOGRAM
  The film produced by x-ray.

S

SALINE
  A solution of salt and water.
SALPINGITIS
  Inflammation of a tube. For example: eustachian salpingitis.
SAPROPHYTE
  An organism that lives on dead or decaying organic matter.
SEBACEOUS GLANDS
  Glands which secrete a greasy lubricating substance.
SEPTOPLASTY
  An operation to straighten the nasoseptum.
SEROUS
  Material which resembles blood serum.
SIMPLE FRACTURE
  A fracture of bone in which the bone does not protrude through the skin.
SPECULUM
  An appliance used to view a passage or cavity in the body. Examples include nasal and ear speculums.

SPHINCTER
  A ring-like band of muscle fibers that constrict a passage or close a natural orifice.
SPONDEE
  Two heavily accented syllables.
SPONTANEOUS
  Occurring without external influence. Such as the spontaneous recovery from an illness.
STAPEDECTOMY
  An operation which includes the removal of the stapes and its footplate, and placement of some form of prosthesis, such as wire, to take the place of the stapes.
STEROID
  A group of compounds that resemble cholesterol. For the most part, these drugs are used for their anti-inflammatory effect. Cortisone is the best known example of this group of medications.
STIMULUS
  Any agent, act, or influence that produces a reaction in the receptor.
STOMATITIS
  Inflammation of the oral mucosa.
STRIDOR
  The wheezing noise present on inspiration or expiration when partial obstruction of the larynx is present.
SUBCUTANEOUS
  Situated or occurring beneath the skin.
SUBEPITHELIAL
  Situated beneath the epithelium.
SUBJECTIVE
  Pertaining to or perceived only by the affected individual.
SUBMUCOUS RESECTION
  Excision of the cartilage of the nasoseptum.
SUPINE
  The position assumed when lying on the back.
SYMPTOM
  Any change in a patient's condition indicative of some bodily or mental state.
SYSTEMIC
  Pertaining to or affecting the body as a whole.

T

THERMAL
  Pertaining to, characterized by heat.
THRESHOLD
  That value at which a stimulus minimally produces a sensation.
TINNITUS
  A buzzing or ringing noise in the ears.
TRANSUDATE
  A fluid substance which has passed through a membrane or has been extruded from a tissue as a result of inflammation.
TRAUMA
  A wound or injury.

TRISMUS
  Difficulty in opening the mouth due to mascular spasms, pain, or disturbance of the 5th cranial nerve.
TUMOR
  Any swelling. It may indicate either inflammation, infection, or neoplasm.
TYMPANOPLASTY
  Surgical reconstruction of the hearing mechanism of the middle ear.

U

UNILATERAL
  Affecting one side only.

V

VENEREAL
  Due to or propagated by sexual intercourse.
VERTIGO
  A hallucination of movement. A sensation as if the external environment is revolving around the patient, or as if the patient were revolving in space.
VESICULATION
  Small circumscribed elevations of epithelium containing a serous liquid.
VIRUS
  One of a group of minute infectious agents which are too small to be seen under a microscope.
VOCALIZATION
  The act of making a sound through the mouth.